CROCHET FOR BEGINNERS

THE MOST COMPLETE STEP BY STEP GUIDE TO
LEARN THE BASICS AND GET STARTED
QUICKLY

PENELOPE COLE

Table of contents

INTRODUCTION

How many crochet forms are there, where did they come from and where do they go? I know of a few types of Crochet most widely used, called Crochet, which involve a number of hook and thread and loop stitches in the west; labeled stitches such as slip stitch, chain stitch, double crochet stitch, half-trip and triple stitch and more.

You can crochet a lot, say from small bags to jackets and sweaters. There are numerous options available. Crochet pattern publishers also search for pattern testers. Contact various companies and offer patterns for review.

Once you start crocheting and have mastered the essential stitches, there are always a few problems that hinder your work and ruin it. By following these crochet tips, you will ensure that your work is neater and even finished every time you crochet.

Crocheting usually requires a single crochet hook that is a hooked needle, which is used for drawing yarn into knotted loops. Whether you are crocheting a cloth, a clothing item, or an accessory, you will need a few crochet items to get you started. Required crochet supplies may rely on the nature of the design and the commodity.

CHAPTER ONE

What is Crochet?

Crochet is a way to make yarn or crochet thread fabric with a crochet hook. In fact, the word crochet means 'hook.'

When you start a crochet project, you just start with a knot, put the hook through the loop, wrap the yarn around the hook and pull it through the first loop. Keep winding the thread around the hook and drag it over the previous loop before the target duration is achieved. Every loop is considered a chain because it loops around the corresponding loop.

After the chains are made, you can join the last chain with a slip knot to form a circle and work in rounds, or simply turn the chains and work in rows. When you operate in circles, the job is switched around at the end of each section, so if you operate in loops, you have the right to switch. The patterns let you know when and when they won't turn.

Once the yarn is wound around the needle, a crochet stitch is created, and one or two loops are drawn through the chain of stitches from the previous row or circle. The great thing about crochet is that there is only one active loop on the hook at the end of each stitch.

You can produce all kinds of clean textiles with crocheting such as doilies, table cloths, bedding, and afghans. Moreover, it's possible to make your own clothes, something like sweaters, ponchos, skirts, scarves, hats, slippers and headbands. You may also crochet certain pieces, such as pockets, purses, dishcloths, sheets, and servings.

Several videos are available on how to crochet online, especially on sites such as YouTube.com. There are also several free crochet patterns accessible online or in your nearest yarn shop, and you can purchase design books.

Models typically inform you what kind of yarn and what crochet hook size to use. The thick yarn needs a bigger crochet hook, whereas a smaller hook is required for thin yarn or crochet thread.

Learning some ways to crochet can be difficult; the thread must be carried in one eye, and the crochet hook with the other; both must work together to complete the object.

Crocheting will take a lot of time for people who start to crochet, but the pace is improved with daily practice. It can even be stressful at first, but ultimately it's soothing and may also alleviate tension as one with the yarn and handle.

Is Crochet an Art?

Attempts to address the basic problem, "What is art?" have left an incomplete and vulnerable end of the traditional theory of aesthetics. Why, though, do we make matters more complicated when we ask, "How is crochet art?"

Only as crochet is increasingly becoming a modern tool for men and women skilled in what we once deemed "visual arts." It happens in many other fields historically considered "handicrafts," including pottery and weaving. With one artist, you can learn that as the explanation behind their success. Artists speak about an exciting discovery rendered unexpectedly marvelous with the "fresh" crochet fabrics, which operate with one continuous thread and the unexpected directional changes enabled by crochet.

Many artists were quite articulate in this regard. Listen to Janet Decker: "To be completely free in my work is my goal. Crochet has succeeded in that respect as it is virtually unlimited and easily integrated with other media. Although I am using a craft-oriented vehicle, the crochet stitch, I don't deal just with color and design.

And listen to Camillo Capua: "To come up with something and to grasp something in terms of the actual structure helps it to stand and sink against its own power. The versatility of crochet makes it easy to reduce it and respond more practically. Perhaps it's the good thing that the object is created from a string of fiber, maneuvered mathematically, and is only a string when done.

Crochet is not exactly anything modern. It's a lacemaking art that has been home and closets decoration for decades but has evolved only nowadays in its creative application and technological method to the heights embodied by types of nonfunctional art. In contrast to weaving, crochet was never a textile skill that man wants to live.

Crochet, though, is in a crucial manner in its infancy; it has not been deemed a modern frontier; its simplicity allows it an exceptionally appropriate medium for innovation. It is creators that smash laws and crash down the ancient walls of art and design. In short, the controversy about art and craft is becoming increasingly meaningless and trivial.

We also have a long way to go. Crochet as art is still a rich and thrilling topic as it is a truly beautiful illustration of how crafts are to be presented in a different way.

Take your thread, template, and needle, and let's start crocheting, and it's your own craft.

History of Crochet

Nobody really knows when or how to crochet was made. It is because, unlike sewing, Crochet was more a needle art of men-unlike the intricate spinning of lace crafted for empire and the upper class, later saved for research by museums and historians.

Overall the years, Crochet has always remained true to its origins, a more open craft than knitting, with greater flexibility in terms of freedom to make more creative with decorative clothing, hats, afghans, and other ventures.

Historians agree that Crochet was invented by the lower classes. It's hard to imagine today, but sewing needles and fine fabrics and yarns in the early days of the world were available to the very wealthy. This left someone who was bad and desired a good sport. And if such fabrics were available to a growing middle class in Europe, they were only used to knit darn boots.

So a non-recorded underground crochet trend started with people who could locate few loops or fibers and then created decorative nodes and chains using their fingertips. This initial endeavor may have been easier than Crochet to macramé, but it's still an inexpensive and innovative art for masses.

Perhaps about 1300 men started to design hooks out of either bone, brass, wood in Turkey, ivory, or Persia, North Africa, China, and India. However, before people began to "crochet in the air," as it was later called in France in the 1800s, there developed an alternative way of knotting and looping threads.

Since nobody realized that a crochet stitch could render a garment by itself, they switched to a technique called a "tambourine," which was first created in China and involved crochet-like stitches. This was around 1700 that textile makers stretched a backdrop tissue into a frame and then used a hook to move a thread loop into the tissue. Once the next loop was made, the hook was used together, and the first chain stitch was made.

In the middle of the late 1700s, enough of the first Tambor pieces had arrived in Europe from the East to inspire Europeans to learn how to dance. Eventually, fabric is eliminated, and the top class Europeans who mastered tambourine began to produce the first modern Crochet with hooks made of silver, brass, or steel. Naturally, because only the upper class were permitted to Crochet, the masses were left to keep dreaming of more creative socks.

It was only a time before people learned to fashion their own hooks and to take hold of odds and ends of the thread needed to make their own garments adorned. (When it emerged first in Europe, Crochet was not used to creating new clothes because it was used to decorate existing clothes.)

The upper class, who made Crochet trendy, saw and quickly proclaimed the emerging middle class and their new Crochet out of fashion. They quickly got back to the snap that the lower classes could not afford and did not come back to Crochet until

Queen Victoria took her Crochet and made her fashionable again.

Although a more recent type of Crochet came originally from Italy and Spain, the French invented their Crochet in the late 1700s, calling it 'hook' from the Middle French word 'croc.' The French also created the first patterns of clothing by 1842. Crocheted lace is also developed around this time.

Later, standardized patterns were distributed that were easy to follow. While it would take a while to develop standardized needles, by the mid-1800s, Crochet was the easy way for the emerging middle class to take the time in front of the fire while creating unique clothing, accessories, and home decorations.

Modern Crochet remains the people's needle-based craft to this day. It is easy to learn, fun to do, and far less restrictive than its more refined family member. Actually, one of the most experienced crocheters is something called 'random crocheting.'

Random crocheting is the art to create your own original design from a pattern and change it. You can also try to crochet with an idea and only see what happens. This is the magic of Crochet, which what makes it so lovely, rewarding, which soothing in this very new and quickly evolving world.

Beginning Crochet

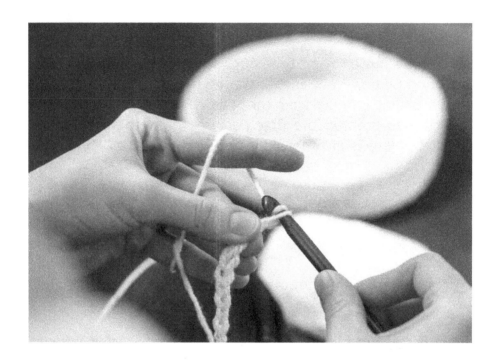

The first step to enjoy this great craft is to buy crochet hooks and yarn. You will learn that crochet hooks are available in various sizes, styles, and colors. The G hook is a good hook size for starting crochet. You should use a G hook for simple stitches. It is recommended.

You might have thought you read a foreign language if you've ever looked at a crochet pattern. That is because crochet styles provide abbreviations to keep it simple and tidy. To start crocheting with a pattern, the abbreviations must be identified, as well as the simple stitches clearly understood. Let's first look at different types of crochet hooks and yarn and talk about the many crochet stitches.

Some crochet stitches are very simple and easy, and all beginners can begin with them. You will quickly note, though, that as your ability improves, you will eventually begin using some of the tougher stitches. It is just amazing to produce results with various stitches, blend stitches and stitches with yarn colors.

When you learn to crochet, the first rule of thumb is to try to have fun. This means that if you make a mistake or don't understand a pattern, you shouldn't be stressed out. Only try making stitches in the thread. Your aim is to create a chain stitch that looks even and uniform.

You can practice your stitches by crocheting different swatches before you even begin to think of tackling your first pattern. These are square-shaped crocheted blocks that can determine how many rows you want, but the object is to practice your stitches until you feel comfortable with their shape and appearance.

Neither should you care about wasting your thread. In fact, if you want, you can save and stitch your swatches together for other projects. It is recommended that you make crochet swats to test your gage before you start other projects. So, relax and enjoy crochet swats; they are the basis for your future crochet designs.

It's also important to know that since your crochet experience is meant to be fun, you may want to test your creativity limits. When you start to save various stitches, you may agree whether you work on a pattern and want to move it in a new direction. Never be afraid to break the habits and checks. You will also find that you should practice and experience and develop your own specific styles. That's how I created some of my favorite patterns.

You can also discover that many lovely crochet pieces can be made from basic forms such as triangles, circles, and rectangles. This was an ideal way for newcomers to relate to a variety of projects without actually having the expertise or the capacity to work with more complicated projects.

However, you will find that just a few basic stitches and the desire to follow a pattern will get you to crochet several projects in a short time.

If you like Afghan, then after mastering the simple stitches, you may want to begin learning Granny Square. Many beginners create a giant Afghan Granny Square with a pillow.

The essential thing is to make sure the time is enjoyable. Enjoy your crochet, and you'll find that you'll crochet like a pro in no time.

An Introduction to Crochet

Crochet is a way to make a lovely lacy fabric that you can use as curtains, panels, and doilies. You can also use crochet technology to make stylish winter accessories like hats, scarves, mitts, and a lot more. If you are excellent at crocheting, you will even make sweaters and other tops that are really trendy to wear anytime.

Since at least the early 1800s, the art of crocheting has been around. There is evidence that it existed even before, but there seems to be no solid evidence as to its origin.

You require thread and a crochet hook to crochet. The hook is basically a thin stick with a small spinning button (hook) to work the yarn through the active loop. Unlike knitting, you normally have only one working loop on your thread, and it is ideal for those who want to deal with the yarn.

In order to start a crochet project, you begin with a knot on your thread. Then you wrap the yarn over the hook and pull it through the knot. It is also the first row, and essentially you can make as many of those as you need to get the amount you want for your cloth.

You can start working your first row directly into the chains after you have completed the chains. You simply thread the hook into the chain, loop the rope around the hook and draw it through the chain stitch to do so. This is meant to give you two hook loops. Then wrap the yarn over a hook and drag it through both loops for the last time. This is known as the single crochet stitch, one of the easiest stitches to make. There are many other crochet stitches you can use similarly to create lovely lace.

You should work in rows or in circles and work in the previous rows or circles. If you work in rows, you must turn your work on the end of each row, and if you work in rounds, it is a common way to attach a slip stitch to each round.

If you do not know how to crochet, the easiest way to practice is to crochet basic patterns for crochet beginners. Another thing that can make you learn better is to take a few moments to study the abbreviations of crochet and how to decipher crochet instructions or crochet graphs. Both are very easy to understand, and learning to read can allow you to discover the crochet art even more quickly.

Art of Crochet

In the early 1800s, lace fabrics were much more costly than crochet goods. Throughout Europe, some groups use crochet products to define their social standing, showing simply that they could afford crochet products or other lace items. The crocheting business only requires cheaper supplies and materials, which are usually threads and yarns that you can buy in nearby markets.

Many assume that in countries such as Saudi Arabia, China, and Brazil, crocheting and knitting have evolved. This theory was developed due to the cultural tradition of clothing used by people living in these countries. Many experts often claim that crochet art is more relevant than the need to manufacture crochet and knitted goods to bend the forefinger.

During the early years of colonization, crocheting was regarded as the primary subsistence of people living in towns and cities in the western part of Europe. Some royalties allow the use of a crochet commodity to symbolize wealth and strength. Crocheting and sewing are the joy of many during these days. It has evolved as an art of creating excellent crochet crafts and designs.

A person can purchase a variety of yarns and threads to make a crochet product. Depending on the type of pattern or design he will produce, he can choose different textures and colors. There are actually specific varieties of yarn on the market. He may find baby/fingering, weight loss, sweetheart, sports/baby, and bulky types of yarns commonly used in knitting and crocheting.

Yarns are usually classified by their styles to assess the consistency of the yarn. It helps to determine which specific yarn is appropriate for a particular crochet product. In addition, the number of skeins, care orders, thickness, and the fiber content of the yarns will also be known to a person.

Here are some other supplies besides the yarn needed to create a crochet product.

1. The knitting needles are very important for crocheting. They are usually straight materials made from aluminum, wood, and plastic. They can be used in different sizes from 2 mm to 15 mm. They are bought in pairs with a button and pointed edges. This design was designed to prevent the needle from sliding when left on the unfinished crochet product.

2. The crochet hooks are used to capture the thread loops used to crochet. They often derive the loosening and slipping stitches from the stitches of the thread. We are also made of titanium, plastic, and wood. The wooden crochet hooks are the most frequently used when making a crochet product, as their fingers are easier to handle and are also considered the cheapest.

3. The pattern diagram is very important to create a crochet product. This is a reference to how he implements the directions and concept sketches. Most patterns are usually easy to follow, particularly when the person is highly qualified to crochet. For most beginners, patterns are easier and more common. You are designed primarily to learn and appreciate basic crochet goods designs.

4. He will also require other tools, such as books and magazines, to provide him with simple crocheting instructions. In case he wants to use various designs for making a crochet hat, crochet blanket, crochet scarf, crochet bag, and other pieces, he-use instructional charts.

5. Special materials are often required to produce special crochet items. Dentures and doilies made of stainless steel crochet hooks must be used. These particular hooks also have a different size than normal wooden hooks.

Crochet products are primarily designed for the joy of fashion. These can be shown in exhibitions in particular where the equipment and resources used are crochet products approved. The quality of the crochet product will also depend on how quickly a person has made it. Some only work on crochet products because of their own pleasure and satisfaction in finishing a specific pattern, the application of their skills to generate income remains helpful.

More About Crocheting

Knitting is one of those activities that seems a lot easier than it actually is. You might ask a friend or family member who knits/crochets to show you how. If you don't know anybody, you might want to participate in or join a social group at the nearest community college.

Knitting and crocheting (and also knitting and cricketing themselves) are without prejudice or prejudice, and something in the knitter and crocheter longs for warming others during difficult times. Even if the craftsman makes a difference to the art, only good will eventually come from it. The knit crochet stockinet is distinct from the knit hook stockinet. While crochet storages can be made in various ways, it is unrealistic to expect that they will act as though they were knit.

Size adjustments are then made by adding or removing the stitch counts in each of the clothing models. Add these towels of toppers to ordinary towels and provide them with a brand-new look! This pattern gives you two different ways to attach your towel. Advanced crochet will render your wonderful stuff with very fine yarn as beautiful lace. For the beginner, though, one of the advantages of this hobby is that it is very economical to start up because the tools you will need at the beginning are cheap and few.

The crochet pattern in rows is charted row by row. It starts with the baseline. There are numerous and varying ones. Including blankets created by mixing several motifs to those in one piece

Anyone sewing wants to sew better. Whatever the idea is, you want it to look incredible, as if you purchased it from a professional designer. Everyone wants to stop working for a full-time crochet design career. While some people can make a living from architecture, the rest see it as a second income.

Understanding when and why you do such things increases trust and makes crocheting effective. Understanding that will help you decide if your company should be put on the market.

All in crochet is difficult with one of the basic stitches. It's like doing algebra, and you have to add, deduct, measure, and divide as you learn math. Anything that can be cleaned and used regularly and makes a beautiful and versatile cloth.

You can really do a lot with double and triple stitches of crochet! When you look at most patterns (plus, of course, the single point), it's the yarn that usually displays the appeal.

Everything will be bought and paid for. And the oxygen for which you breathe must be charged. All the roses come up with this lovely array of knit and crochet flowers. You may find the best way to use yarn scraps or to use new yarns to decorate garments, shoes, bags, and ceilings, adorn home accessories, or create a stunning bouquet as an interesting show item.

Crochet - What Is It? Where Did It Come From and When?

Crochet (pronounced cro-sh-A) is the same method as knitting but involves many needles to draw yarn loops over certain loops.

Crocheting normally involves a single crochet hook, a needle with a hook, which is used to draw thread across knotted loops. If you crochet a rug, a fabric item, or an ornament, you need some crochet supplies to get you started. The difficulty of the design and the product produced depends on the appropriate crochet supplies.

Simple materials of crochet

The simple crochet supplies required would be a crochet needle and a thread; however, the ability to create more complex objects could lead to needles of different kinds, yarns, more complicated designs, instructional books, beads, loops, tape measuring, pompon circle and other materials that will enhance and embellish the crochet object.

Crochet Hooks

Crochet hooks are distributed in several styles, which typically suit the length of the yarn used. Crochet products may be crafted of fiber, copper, wood, bone, among other things, including crochet hooks. Crochet hooks vary by size and maybe in millimeters from 3.5 to 0.4, numbers from 00 to 16, or letters from B to S.

The crochet hook design you will use differs from the crochet form and template. Tunisian crochet hooks are stretched, and the last section of the handle has a stopper; a variant of the Tunisian hook is the Cro-hook with a double end hook that allows double-sided crochet using two threads of the same color.

Any people with arthritis or medical complications may require ergonomically built crochet hooks. The bottom line is to still buy the finest crochet hooks you can afford.

Components for Crochet

Some crochet fabrics are commonly considered to come in increasing thicknesses and textures as fabric or string. These types are bulky weights, which are used for heavy and warm clothes; weight wore on scarves, sweaters, and mittens; weight sport is used for sweaters and baby items and weight fingering for lighter items such as socks, lightweight weights, and certain baby items; these are the main crochet yarns for the production of most items. You may produce yarn fabrics of acrylic, fur, alpaca, cotton, silk, cashmere, and a lot more than that.

Supplies and tools for crochet

Instruction books are a prerequisite for beginners, whereas advanced patterns are used to create more complicated clothes and other products. Whether you are a beginner or expert at crocheting depends on the amount of crochet supplies required.

Do You Want to Learn to Crochet?

Have you been thinking about crochet learning? Many people told me they 'd like to be able to crochet, but they fear it'd be too difficult for them to learn. To learn, you don't know anything about yarn, hooks, or even how to start.

Actually, crochet isn't hard at all. It's hard only if you think it's, so you must change your mind. Looking at the crochet fundamentals.

Have you ever seen kids (or maybe you did) this yourself) playing with a yarn or string piece? They are They let a knot fall in the thread or string with your fingers, then make a loop and cross the first loop.

In one loop, another loop, and so on. That's the same thing as the key start of the crochet line, but you Instead of your fingers, a crochet hook.

How do you pick your yarn? When you pick your thread, the basic types are five: baby/fingering, sports weight/baby, Weight worsted, chunky and bulky. Degraded Weight is a better beginner kind.

Fingering and baby yarns are very good; sporty is generally three plies (ply means the number of strands twisted to shape the yarn together). Deforested Weight is a four-fold yarn. Small and bulky are More heavy yarns.

Yarns may be constructed of natural or synthetic fibers.

Acrylics are popular and easy to use Wash. Cotton yarns are easy to use and make big crocheted dishcloths a simple one project for beginners. For beginners.

You want to stay away from a beginner use fur yarns and fuzzy yarns. They 're soft and smooth Very nice, but harder to work with as it your stitches are hard to see. You should test it later, improving your crocheting skills.

Just look at the labels to choose your yarn. They are you 're going to teach you what you need to know. A few yarns get only free mark trends. You're going to be, and those in your pattern set want to save if you don't want to fix the object now. Creating a pattern set is always fantastic for use later.

Next, you're going to pick your anchor. Are aluminum, plastic, wood, or steel can be made. Steel hooks are very small and are used for good work like lace and doilies.

As a beginner, you learn the worn out.

Weight wool for an H (5.00 mm), I (5.5 mm) or hook J (6.00mm). You 're learning to crochet would like to build a collection of the many hook sizes.

The problem I found most beginners is having the thread and the loop to work together. Yet this is the case training makes good for everything. It's not important much until you hang it, and you are in its flow.

You should do something before you actually make an item.

Work bits. Play bits. Start to make a chain of 15 twenty chains. You do this by wrapping a slip knot yarn and loop pulling around your finger, then put the knot of slip on your hook. Pull the two yarn ends to tighten and adjust the knot slip. Then, bring your yarn back to front over your hook, grab the yarn with your hand, and pull the string on your line hook. Repeat until 15 to 20 chain stitches are available.

Now you are using the single crochet (sc) to make your own the trial piece. Research piece. In your hook 's second chain (Just count off the hook two chains) and insert your chain collar. Your chain locks. Put your yarn across the hook and draw that yarn through the chain stitch. There are now two hook loops.

Bring your yarn from behind to front over the hook and draw it on the hook through both loops. There remains one loop on the hook. On the lock. You ended your first single crochet stitch. Crochet stitch.

Repeat the single crochet point until the end link lines. Link lines. When you started with twenty strings, will 19 single crochet stitches in this row as you skipped the first chain and started in your second chain hook.

First, you make the next row of single crochet a chain point by wrapping the yarn over your crochet and pull it on your hook through the loop. Now you are turning your work to make the last sc on the previous one row is at the start now. Make just one crochet in the thread and in each other's thread Past row. Past lines. For every new row, repeat this.

You will notice that two loops are on top of the single crochet stitches completed. You've placed your hook through these two loops. I noticed that an error Some beginners are just going through one Single crochet loop. This is a functioning variation ok in other forms, but later, you will know to improve skills.

Continue to work your sample piece until you for the crochet look. This helps you learn how to hold your hook so that it is easy to take the yarn, and it will also help you get tension On. You may find that you are too loosely crocheting or. At first, too close. You must learn how to exercise to sustain consistent intensity during the project.

Once you practice and feel ready to try a simple pattern, you can make a scarf search online pattern, which is the beginning of most beginners. Or, as already mentioned, dishcloths are simple patterns for beginners. For beginners.

You find everything you need by searching online. To know about crochet. Crochet knows. Free forms, diagrams crochet abbreviations in patterns, charts for patterns sizes of handles, etc.

I'm sure you'll enjoy the experience of your crochet. I consider it is really calming, a huge cure for pain. It's fun to work with various colors and textures of yarn. It's there.

Great to make things for yourself and as gifts family and friends. Friends.

You can do this while watching TV or sitting in the waiting room of a doctor or in the passenger a vehicle. A vehicle. Just get a crochet bag (or crochet) you are ready to go, one yourself).

I hope that this information has helped you. Your decision as a hobby to make crochet.

Learning to Crochet Made Easy

Crocheting is a wonderful pleasure that is really gratifying and useful. The number of projects of crochet that you can make is infinite. The great thing is that the designs will be useful at home or as donations. Crocheting is not only a hobby, but it also has many advantages.

Many crafts and activities can be pretty costly to know. Crocheting isn't at all costly. The tools needed to get started very simple and not expensive, making crocheting a hobby to learn very attractive.

Also, studying how to crochet is just about getting to know a limited collection of rising stitches. Once you have learned to do these basic stitches, it can be quick and unthreatening to start a simple project. Remember, you can want to start with something plain and convenient.

You just need to know how to create loops, single hook, and double hooks to get going, so practice these stitches before you are pretty confident and aim to scale all three regularly. Don't give up if you don't come out right at the beginning.

Once you feel confident with the initial crocheting measures, you should be ready to begin almost any project you want. You'll have your own hats, scarves, blankets and so on ... Only remove the most important ones behind.

Have you also imagined all your savings by creating fantastic and economical gifts for the whole family? What doesn't want a special design created by hands like a large sweater or a warm hat? Baby pieces are some of the most valuable and functional products to produce.

Crocheting is such a satisfying pleasure because it allows you the chance to feel full and comfortable. You will be complimented and admired by your loved ones through your crochet designs.

You will transfer your skills to others around you until you learn to crochet. Most households exchange crochet bits for decades. Crochet heirlooms may be a symbol of honor and heritage in the household.

Crocheting is highly calming and fun. Crochet learning is also simple, rewarding, and beneficial. The great thing is that it helps you to build all sorts of things for the house, family, and friends quite cheaply. Crocheting is a wonderful art to be passed from one generation to the next.

CHAPTER TWO

Understanding Crochet Instructions and Materials

Some people have questioned how to interpret crochet directions. The following information may be useful.

Crochet guidelines are actually not so difficult to follow and read once you get acquainted with the pattern and understanding of every abbreviated symbol.

Recognize to search in the learning each time you see durations or comas for punctuation and pause. The fundamental element in the study of crochet patterns and instruction is to understand the writing style, including crochet abbreviations. However, it is not important to know the symbols and abbreviations immediately, because when needed, you can always refer to your list.

It would be very convenient to have someone by your side reading the instructions clearly at you. While it is not important to remember abbreviations, it is important to understand them so that you know what to do.

The instruction to display sequence repetitions normally uses parentheses) (and asterisks (*).

For example, when the pattern guidelines you to "repeat from *," it is necessary to examine the row instructions you are currently working on and then find the asterisk (*). Crochet the instructions immediately after this asterisk (*).

Sometimes a pattern asks to "repeat from *" not only once, but more. If that is the direction, you will go back, locate the asterisk (*), and crochet the notes, how long the template would be required.

In fact, there is only one asterisk (*) in a row, and the "repeats" should lead you to the end of the row so that there is no extra instruction to complete the repetitions.

Some patterns use a single asterisk (*) in the beginning and at the end of the "repeat." If you hit the successor "single asterisk" (*), you know that this is the location where the "repeat" is interrupted.

At certain times, patterns use 'a single asterisk (*) and a 'double asterisk (**),' where the 'double asterisk (**)' is usually used to indicate where to end the repeat: For example, a pattern will instruct you to 'replay from * to **' and then you must look back in the round instructions and locate the asterisk (*).

Instructions usually require "work only" to work on the same stitch and do not decrease or raise stitches.

These are many things to keep in mind when looking at a pattern of crochet:

1. Crochet patterns and instructions are usually worked in rounds or rows. Whether you do or work in rounds, rows, or a mix of both, every crochet pattern will be specified.

2. Almost every crochet patterns and instructions are generally ranked in regarding to the difficulty, such as advanced, intermediate, easy, or beginner. Chooses a pattern with a level of difficulty that suits your capabilities in order to avoid frustration in trying to finish a pattern with an advanced level.

3. It is very important to count the stitches when you're on the job, and you can keep track of how many stitches the pattern takes for each round or section.

4. You have to check your jacket at all times. To do that, crochet a sample about 4 x 4 inches in size in the pattern that is used for your crochet instructions. If your jacket is greater than that shown by the pattern, use a smaller hook; try a much bigger hook if your jackets are smaller.

5. Registering for a crochet course can be very helpful when you start learning crochet.

When you just start off, never be disappointed if you cannot understand every pattern and abbreviations. You will be constantly practical in reading and understanding crochet patterns.

Begin with simple projects, such as dishcloth, fox, pot holding, or any easy or small patterns, where you think you can understand the instructions. The satisfaction and self-satisfaction with every finished project or object inspire you to create different patterns at every level, and you will soon grow and can make differences.

To understand enough about Crochet instructions helps reduce the apprehensive factor. If you apply what you have learned about Crochet instructions, don't worry.

Where to Find Help in Learning How to Crochet

Though some crochet is going to pick up among the younger generations, many new crocheters are often alone while wanting to study how to crochet. There is a lot involved in learning how to crochet, and it can be extremely confusing and even frustrating for those who don't get the luxury to look over the back of someone else.

YouTube alone has thousands of free crochet tutorials, not to take into account all the crochet pattern web pages. In addition to all great video tutorials, many designers have taken the extra miles and even put many of their patterns on a video to enable new beginners to pursue the whole project.

Videos can be excellent when displaying all the steps involved with the stitches as well as the patterns and thus helps to create a lot of confusion and/or frustration from the beginner. In the long run, however, the view of video for each project can take quite considerable time.

To any crochet novice, the above can be daunting. It is, therefore, important that you spend a lot of time reading and studying art before you even try.

And where will beginners go for assistance? There are other options. All who can afford to invest in a crochet-for-starter book or at least are able to make such a buy. These books are generally informative and answer any questions a beginner may not have thought about asking. It will be the least frustrative direction.

All the questions, hints, and videos that can be found in a crochet book for beginners can also be found online free of charge. The only difference in which you will have to search online for these answers, which will take longer in the end. It could also be more confusing because not only the internet is loaded with information, but many crochet stitches and techniques are made by different crocheters differently. As a result, people learning to crochet could be confused about the correct method.

Online crochet directories have a huge range of online photo and video tutorials. This is a perfect spot to go to when a pattern needs a stitch you haven't played with.

The Handmade Yarn Council and Catalog of Annie also have an outstanding guide on how to learn crochet patterns. Google will quickly search for them.

An abbreviation chart in crochet is another thing a beginner might want to read before starting to crochet. Once, a fast Google search will pull up one.

Once the basics are down, you can start looking for a crochet pattern for beginners and start crocheting. The best way to go for the first few projects is through a simple project. Dishcloths, hats, and scrubbers are good places to start with.

The key to learning how to crochet is to crochet for at least a couple of minutes each day, until you can easily hold the hook and yarn. If it becomes too hard at any time, it could help to put the project down for a little and return to it later on. Training is fine, as in everything.

Learning How to Use Crochet Instructions

Trying to learn how to crochet can be a wonderful experience which rewards you with lifelong knowledge and relaxation outlet. Focusing on crochet means that there's little room to focus on so much else; in turn, every clutter, as well as noise from a chaotic and busy day, is all of a sudden relegated to the back burner.

Crochet patterns for some specific projects can be found in several local design shops, as well as online. Make sure that you use a beginner's template that includes common stitching, easy form, and unadorned lines while trying to finish a project with crochet directions.

First and foremost, when choosing your project and buying your crochet instructions, read the crochet instructions several times to make sure that you have a thorough understanding of your steps. In most cases, a shortcut key is included with all crochet instructions that help you decipher the directions.

Often check at the crochet instructions and figure out which items you need for the project. Make sure you have adequate resources and finish the job; the last thing you need to do when you're in the midst of a project is to go out for more yarn. Often, if you're dealing with other colors, you can't promise that you can fit the yarn perfectly.

Most crochet directions contain something called a gage guide, which is some sort of realistic area where you can crochet any stitches. Which means which your stitch matches in with the stitch measures needed in the crochet directions to save you some irritation.

With that, you are able to continue the project with the step-by-step guidance of the crochet directions. Take some time and concentrate on the method. Note precision is not required. When you complete more and more crochet projects, you can find it simpler to obey the tutorial for crochet and produce the desired results.

Learn How to Crochet - A Beginner's Guide to Crocheting

So, what exactly is crocheting? It is a way of making fabric from thread or yarn using a tool called a crochet hook. There are several different threads and yarns and endless numbers of assorted hooks on the market. Works by dragging thread loops or yarn through a set of adjacent loops. It could sound easy, and it really is. Nonetheless, you need some creativity and the ability to do it well. You must also have the right hooks, yarns, and manuals. Like something, you might end up messing up your hard work from the beginning if you don't pay attention.

The secret of good crochet is to make sure that you select a project with good instructions. When you do this, you'll find it all too much better. This is because good instructions provide you with details like the right yarn and hook to use and how to make the right points. Many people think they can simply dive in without good instructions, and the end result is not nice!

Instructions are necessary, and it is crucial that you first know all the fundamentals of crocheting. Many directions use shorthand and abbreviate terms like double crochet DC and single crochet SC, etc. If you do not know these terms, you will not understand the instructions, and your results will be terrible.

Many people ask how different crocheting and knitting are. The answer is simple. Knitting requires two hooks while only one is required for crochet. It is due to the fact that crocheting has only one stitch involved during a sequence of continuous stitches. It can be the end of the dream if you knit a thread, but with crochet, it is not such a tragedy.

More information can be found in my signature. You will find here a review of a fantastic resource that teaches you everything you ever need to know about crocheting.

The Difference in Knitting and Crochet

People often confuse crochet and knitting. Most of the time, when someone sees someone crocheting, they believe they knit. The word knitting has been around for decades, and people still experience knitting as they see wool and crochet or needle. Yet more people learn how to crochet than knit is the amusing thing.

Knitting is two crafts' older. I believe you can find almost the beginning of clothes knitting and weaving. It was called a man to work at the beginning of knitting. But over time, it changed more frequently than not to be the boys. Nowadays, there are many talented male designers, but still, women are the majority of knitters.

Crochet's just a few hundred years old. I believe it came more like embellishment for clothing than for clothing itself. Yet over time, the talented people began to work with hook and yarn beautiful things.

Some of the differences between crochet and knitting are:

1. 1 Knitting utilizes two pointing needles
2. 2 Crochet using a thread with a crochet edge
3. 3 Spinning with the central stitches

Crochet primary stitches are single and double crochet stitches.

3 Knitting has the stitch side and the stitch side

Crochets got a good and incorrect hand.

Each design requires any form of yarn. Thread spinning is the same as thread crocheting. However, crochet thread is used for both crochets, however, knit doilies and tops. We use all sorts of fabric to deal with and often very inventive to knit bags to belts. You never learn about such things spinning.

Knitting makes the yarn softer and sleeker than crochet. Crochet typically makes a chunkier piece, and you'll see crochet if it's used more frequently than not in blankets. Yet also beautifully made baby things are crocheted again.

You may create everything from tiny, delicate flowers to big Afghans with crochet or knit. Crochet thread bedspreads are only lovely yet time-consuming. A beautiful knitted baptismal fabric is a glorious gem and transmitting descendants. You can crochet or knit warm winter hats, comfortable slippers, and shawls in order to keep the chill-out or to make a lacquer vest.

Yeah, you can make lovely presents for everyone with needle, hook, and yarn or string. It is a pleasure that can be as affordable or pricey as the budget requires. Crochet or knit is an art worth knowing and transferring to the next century.

Surprisingly, 80% of knitters are even willing to crochet. However, only approximately 30 percent of crocheters can knit.

Patterns in Red Heart Yarn

When you just start and want to live as cheap as possible, search the labels on the yarn sheets. They have some really cool crochet and knitting designs. We even rate the patterns, so you will consider simple patterns or start patterns to continue.

CHAPTER THREE

Top 10 Crochet Tips and Tricks

Exactly does this mean how other people are making their crochet creations so beautiful? When part of a project has to do with practicing, certain tips can be used to develop your crochet skills. -- you 're only beginning to know how to crochet or years, here are ten tips that you can continue to use today! Learn how to use yarns, how to spin yarns, how to make new stitching, and more.

1. Do you like to crochet, because you have young children and you find it difficult to get enough time for your hobby? Why not involve them? You enjoy it, so you will spend time

with your mother and support her too. Let your kids find little crochet motivations for you or show them how to crochet their doll scarves. Only note to still have a hook and a thread in the vicinity to prevent stopping and searching.

2. In the same project, avoid mixing different yarn types. Specific yarns, such as cotton and acrylics, can shrink when washed at varying speeds. The effect is that your crochet creation, which looked so perfect once done, would appear blurred and worn out until cleaned.

3. Should you just look for a simple way to wound your yarn in the right ball? Only tie the thread between two inches. Take your fingers out of the ball as you do. You've got the right ball now because the friction is loose, and the thread won't spill out. Moreover, if you drop it because it's soft, the ball won't roll away.

4. Use post-it notes to track your progress while you are working on a project. When each line is finished, move the post-it note to the next line and never lose your spot. You should also make notes or keep track of the number of repeats you did on the post-note. Once it is complete, just start using a new one. Also, if you discover mistakes or modify the pattern, you can type them in the post-it note and keep them in that place when using the pattern in the future again.

5. To keep your crochet project smooth and clean, thread the tail ends of your yarn into your project as you work. One approach is to use a cotton needle to thread the fabric in, making it very secure and unworkable. Use the needle

threader to make the yarn on the needle easier. Another approach is to use a crochet hook that is 2 or 3 times thinner than the one that you used. The smaller hook lets you easily weave the yarn between your project stitches.

6. An easy way to creating new stitches is just to insert your hook in the previous row under the two stitch loops. This way, you already have a loop on your hook when finishing a stitch, making it easier to continue the next stitch. Never include the stitch still on the hook when counting how many stitches you have finished in that row.

7. You can use plastic divided ring markers to track special stitches or the end of a row on your crochet project. You should also use security locks, discarded yarn in a different color or twist links, whether you have one, or if you run away from them. We all work the same way, and if you do have these things on hand, you can save time.

8. Many patterns provide directions on the same line in the pattern for many different sizes using parentheses. In order to keep track of the scale, simply highlight or circle the chosen scale before beginning the sequence. So, you won't accidentally begin to follow the wrong size instructions.

9. Many people find the winter months dull due to the cold and sunshine. Work with bright colors that are fun and lively to help cheer you up. Always make sure that you spend in a positive light when you are working.

10. If you work with a pattern that sometimes switches colors, like making a checkerboard effect, don't start and stop every

color every time you move. Simply keep the color going through the previous row and stitch over the yarn. When the pattern calls for a change in color, the new color is ready to use. Moreover, you don't need to weave in the tail ends of the yarn with this method.

Eight More Essential Crochet Tips

Once you have started crocheting and perfected the simple stitches, there are still few problems that impede your development and spoil your job. By following these crochet tips, any time you crochet, you can ensure you finish your job more neatly and evenly.

Tip 1: Not enough room for round work.

Sometimes it does not appear like there is enough room to work all the correct stitches on the middle ring while working around. Do not work over the top of the previously working stitches if you have this problem; instead, do the following:

1. Adjust the last loop on the line and drop the handle.
2. Move the stitches up softly from the bottom of the circle, making space at the end of the round.
3. Attach your Hook again, close the string, and crochet.
4. Repeat this cycle until the round is done.

Tip 2: Unintended work holes or stretched stitches.

Often you find that you have some gaps that may not be there in your crochet, or some of the stitches seem to have stretched out when they seem to be pulled in the next step. The explanation is typically simple; in the previous row, you won't crochet into the correct part of the thread.

To fix this, always ensure that you have crossed the two loops of the stitch after putting your Hook into the stitch in the line below, unless the layout tells you otherwise, as in loopy hole designs.

Tip 3: Break frames.

Don't just abandon it if you find a broken thread. This makes the job look very bad, as it leaves little stitches on the pattern that is visible and detracts from the true nature of crochet. The time it takes to rectify these split points is praised by having a clean and orderly appearance at work.

When you find a split stitch and break your crochet thread, undo all and split stitch, reinsert your thread and continue crocheting once again. It's worth the extra effort!

Practice 4: Found it tough to crochet in the base section.

Any crochet project's first line is also the hardest. Particularly if you use very thin yarn and a very thread, it can be very hard to crochet into a chain line!

If you find it challenging to crochet the first row, attempt to crochet the base row with a hook larger than that needed for the design, it would break the base row of the chain and make the stitches a bit wider. It does not show the final result, and it will help you put the usual Hook in the right section of the multiple chain stitches.

Vice 5: Starting to curl crocheting.

If you work using the straight-line method, if you think the work starts curling in the first few squares, that is because of the anxiety. You crocheted the row of the base tighter than the rest of the design. You have two ways to solve this:

1. Using a crochet hook one size larger than the Hook used to crochet the pattern.
2. Using the same size anchor, but loosen the job (foundation row).

Vice 6: Difficult to see where to crochet.

It is hard to see exactly what part of the stitch you will crochet in when you learn first to crochet, especially if you use dark-colored yarn. So, when you start to crochet, you use light-colored yarns and needles, which make it easier to see the stitches. Move towards darker colors as your experience and trust rises.

Tip 7: Stitches missing.

Counting the stitches is one of the biggest strategies for good crocheting. It's also one of the most common problems to find that you have fewer pads after crocheting a row than the pattern says or that you keep using a crochet pattern if you don't. The most frequent mistake is to lose stitches in the early and/or later stages. This is because the first or last point of a row is omitted. And if you're in this place, test your origins and ends before looking at the row 's body!

Tip 8: Tapering rectangular work inside or outside.

This problem stems from the previous problem and is due to stitches that can go up or down without knowing it! You should count your stitches regularly to make sure that no stitches are missed or increased inadvertently. The most common mistake is to miss or add stitches once again at the beginning or end of the garments so it should be tested before the row body can be inspected.

Many of those tips are ideally helpful for your next crochet attempt. Having these things in mind will make the crocheting itself look more polished and smoother as you take the crochet hook up.

Learning the Craft of Crocheting - The Crochet Pattern

Crochet is for grandmothers! That's most people's thinking about crocheting. In fact, however, this is incredibly incorrect.

It's not only not achieved by the disabled, but not by other others. It's also done in other designer clothes.

Crocheting is not just for our grannies and bitter spinsters. It can be done by all. Particularly, now that clothing patterns are more inclined to crocheted items, famous garment designers are still struck by Crochet.

Yet crocheting is not exclusively for Jane. One must have the patience and, of course, the time to Crochet something. And how do you really learn to crochet?

It's not too hard to know. Yet it's not an easy one either. What you need is a decent crochet hook, thread, measuring tape, thread needle, pins, and a lot of dedication to complete a crocheting project.

Here are a few hints on how to practice Crochet easily:

Keep the yarn like a pro.

Holding a yarn could be a tricky job for newbies in crocheting. Also, if it just takes a moment to get used to it, it should not be forgotten to learn how to use it properly and skillfully.

This may not be the best thing to learn in the world, but it sure is worth it. The superb job you can do with Crochet is fantastic. When you have any spare time to the hobby of this, you won't miss it.

Here's the way:

1. Once you hold the yarn through your fingers. First, the little finger behind the ring finger, just between the forefinger and middle finger.

2. Another way to catch the thread is through the small finger area and then cross the forefinger.

3. Imagine how you can hold a pencil or spoon while holding the handle. That's how it ought to be maintained. This won't be tough for you to carry the thread from your fingertips down to the hook string.

As you start to Crochet and hang up, you will find your special and most relaxed way to work with your yarn. Don't be afraid to try a new strategy. This will help you become an effective crochet craftsman in the long term.

Size matters when the hook and yarn are reached.

The ability to find the best hook and thread to use in any crochet project should not be taken for granted.

Hooks are identified by various letters and numbers that match certain sizes. The larger the number or letter of the knot, the stronger the knot is when crocheting. As for yarns, names reflect their variations.

Resize the Crochet Scheme

It is as easy as deducting some stitches in order to reduce the scale of a frame. One can miss a stitch in a row and move on to decrease the project scale. It is easy to insert more stitches in a row to extend a project. Two stitches of the same row can be easily joined together. This allows one to create a solo stitch in the next row before it.

Reading a book like a pattern.

The abbreviations of a pattern will confuse the activities of one engaged in crocheting. The use of memory and reasoning will help a great deal to resolve this tiny crochet barrier. The effect of these important abbreviations being able to memorize is a much quicker speed in crocheting and stronger hands.

1. Crochet designs and instructions are typically done in loops or arcs. It is seen on the chart whether you work or work in circles, rows, or combination.

2. Crochet patterns and instructions can usually be graded by level of complexity, such as advanced, complex, simple, or novice. Choose a pattern that matches your skills to a difficulty level. Then through the difficulty level as the skill progresses.

3. Count the stitches you have created during your work to track the correct stitches in each round or row according to the pattern.

4. Check the gage by crocheting a sample in the pattern of about 4 x 4 inches. If your size is bigger than the size of the standard, then use a greater hook; if your size is smaller, then use a bigger hook.

When it's time for you to do a crochet project, make sure you obey the directions well and make your endurance a little sturdy. Prepare your tools in advance to guarantee that your crocheting attempt runs smoothly.

Now you know the crocheting measure. You may not be a master at this time, but at least you should learn the basics. You will now continue working with this little passion for doing great research. Now, come to Crochet!

Common Crochet Stitch Guide

Check this crochet stitch guide for the most increasing crochet stitches. These stitches are crochet building blocks. Once you learn to crochet, you first master these stitches before you move on to patterns.

A stitch of the pattern consists of ordered stitches, which repeatedly create texture, shells, clusters, and decorative patterns. You are using pattern stitches to make crocheted pieces, including scarves, hats, clothes, etc.

Pattern stitches can be found in crochet books or pattern flyers and on the internet. You may use various crochet hooks, even yarns, to learn to create unique written patterns. A stitch pattern could be as simple when two or twelve rows. A row counter will help you monitor your location.

Stitches for Pattern Crochet

Texture crochet patterns use fundamental crochet stitches to make several lightweight designs.

A combination of two chains plus two is used for turning the alternate thread. Start by making a chain as long as you need, turn it, and make two single crochet chain after missing three chains (the turning chain). Then skip a chain and chain one. Then skip chain three. Repeat that in the last point or row, make two single hooks in the last point, row two, and turn. The second row makes the two crochet stitches in the chain spaces and, in the previous row, skip and chain the two hooks. These two rows form a pattern that looks like a leaf when made up.

The double stitch is comparable to the alternating stitch, but it spans two stitches instead of making two single hooks in one stitch. Insert your crochet hook in the thread, loop your yarn around it and then make a hook out and put it into the next row. Fasten over so that you pull a little loop back and then pull the yarn on the hook around all three loops. Repeat the double stitch on each row of stitches. This pattern makes a warm baby blanket with soft, washable crochet yarn.

Many stitches with texture include:

- Up and down, alternating between single and double stitches.

- Checkerboard design, which is made of three or four single, then double crochet stitches, alternating groups.
- Woven stitch made by crocheting a definite diagnosis stitch in a chain, chaining one and skip the next stitch, and then crocheting one. Repeat it in the first row, then crochet one in the previous row 's chain space, skip and chain one on each of the previous row crochets.
- Diagonal stitch that uses long, three-stitch, or double-stitched stitches.

Many more texture stitches are available. Once you have tried a few, you will start to come up with your own textures.

Stitches for Shell or Fan Pattern

The fan or shell stitch is amongst the most popular baby coats, throws and afghans designs. A shell is a group of three to five points that have been worked into a single point or chain. The party will be clustered at the bottom then spread over the edges so that everybody looks like a fan or a seashell.

A single shell has a double hook in one stitch, then two duplicate crochets, a single chain, and two additional double hooks in the next stitch. In the next stitch is another double crochet, but the loop crosses three skips, and a smaller fan is made. Each big shell is crocheted in the shell underneath it and produces a punched bottom.

Shell variations can be made whilst also crocheting small bullets in narrow chain areas, creating an open, delicate design suitable for baby clothes or sheets. By making massive shells over large open areas, an arch-like pattern can be created. Make a fan open up over an opening, and you will have a lovely pattern of starburst.

Crochet Stitch Patterns Cluster

The best-known stitch of the cluster is probably the bobble stitch. The bobble is usually made by making the yarn over and put the crochet needle into the base of your bobble, and pulling a loop out. Instead, you make another thread, pulling the yarn on the hook through two of the stitches. This is coming five times in the base stitch, which ensures that six loops remain on the thread. all six loops are pulled through the yarn to make the bobble and then secured with single crochet in the following stitch.

The pineapple stitch is another famous cluster pattern. Worked on a maximum of two plus four, the pineapple is created by the thread, the hook is inserted into a single stitch, and a four-fold loop is pulled, creating a thread. Draw the crochet yarn through 8 loops, then make a new yarn and pull the yarn into the last two loops. In contrast to bobbles, ananas is often not definite diagnosis stitches tied. Rather, a stitch is cut between every pineapple, and over the skipped stitch, a chain is formed. The pineapples are produced in the next row between the pineapples in the last row. The top of the apple is skipped, and a chain over it is made.

Basic Crochet Stitches

The chain stitch, slip stitch, twin crochet stitch, and triple stitch is among the most common crochet stitches. It is necessary to be comfortable and able to shape these stitches since most crochet patterns contain them all. Nonetheless, you can and make encounter patterns that either skip the triple or the double crochet point, so it is crucial that you know at least one of these specific points. But, it's not long until you feel the need to include them in your arsenal of crochet abilities.

To start crocheting, it is necessary to start from the start place. This is accomplished when the yarn circles into a looped ring, and you put the hook in the loop and take the yarn back up with your hook through the looped ring and tighten the slip knot in your hook. The next step is to place your crochet hook in a manner that suits you, either as a pen or as a knife, with your usual dominant hand and keeps your yarn tightly under your slip knot in your free side.

The chain stitch is the first crochet stitch used for all patterns, which provides either a line or circular crochet with a foundation line or ring. It's an incredibly basic stitch abbreviated in crochet patterns as ch.

Wrap your yarn around your hook (two loops on your thread) to create a sequence of chain stitches, then pull your thread through the first loop. You now only have one loop on your hook, and you have formed one chain stitch. Repeat this cycle with as many chain points as required for your own crochet design or creation.

You will connect the stitches in a slip stitch while you crochet in the round (circular garments such as caps and pins and squares are created in this way). A slip stitch in crochet designs is an abbreviated toss. This is quite clear. Just put the hook into the center of the crocheted first line, gather the yarn and draw the hook again and place two loops on the thread. Draw the hook through the hook's first loop. There is only one loop on the hook, and the work is joined in a ring.

The double crochet stitch that is abbreviated as dc or the single crochet stitch in America is somewhat close to the above-mentioned slip point. The hook is therefore put in the next thread. This depends on what project you are doing. After the thread is placed, stack up the yarn and pull the thread out of the stitch and put two loops on the handle. Now tie the yarn around the handle again and make three loops on the thread. Draw the thread at last through all the loops to remove the one loop on the line with a double crochet stitch.

The last simple crochet stitch we deal with is the triple stitch, which is abbreviated in crochet designs, and which is often regarded as double crochet in America. This is the most difficult of essential crochet stitches and is crochet meat and vegetables since many specialized stitches and methods are based on this thread. It is also a safe practice to execute this crochet stitch effectively.

Wrap the thread around the hook before putting the hook into the position where you like the triple position. Catch the thread and take the loop out of the stitch. You should have three loops on your hook at this stage. Wrap the yarn again around the crochet and make four loops on the needle. Draw the hook through the second and third loops on your hook and leave you on your hook with two loops. Cover the yarn in three loops around the crochet and pull the hook through the remaining loops, leaving you with just one loop and one triple form.

You now have the basic crochet techniques, as we covered the fundamental crochet stitches. You would be shocked how many designs and projects with just a small amount of crochet experience are already accessible to you. Please don't just take my word and search for yourself! And note, have fun! And note!

Much More Than Shamrocks and Lace

Irish baptismal robes feature inspiring designs and handicraft generations. Celtic baptismal gowns look magnificent with fractured shamrocks and Cluny jewelry. Their charming Irish style allows flexibility although it is traditional. The baptismal costumes that have shamrock lace, a shamrock inset or other shamrock details. Victorian lace, Irish lace or Venice lace can be found in the robes.

Celtic crosses, Claddagh, Celtic knot or any other Celtic symbolism can be included in Irish symbols. Irish Christian wedding gowns are embellished, just like Celtic wedding gowns, with 'shingles' (the Irish lace embellishments, brothers and ribbons). Some Irish parents have family crests or wearers' names broken on the baptismal cloth, cape or blanket. The Irish Tower symbolizes pureness, happiness, confidence and fresh existence.

Spanish Catholic Town Spanish

Stakeholders

The shamrock is one of the most prominent and influential icons in Ireland. The shamrock normally adorns the Irish Christian clothes as a sign of the Trinity. The shamrock may be woven into the cloth or put on the gown at one or more places.

Shamrocks, whether green or white, can decorate everything from baptismal clothes and rompers to headbands and bibs.

Satin robes with organza overlay may have scattered shamrocks and small pearls. Often the bodice of an Irish baptismal costume has broken shamrocks.

Bodice, collar, and top of a christening dress may be covered with a decorative shamrock border. So multiple shamrocks, you may have a baptismal dress or only handful-including robes with only one shamrock. A sweet boy's gabardine will have shamrocks and clovers smashed on his chest in the sailor-style, christening romp. The corresponding Christian hat can also be a shamrock.

Lace

Irish baptismal dress contains all kinds of splinters from French lace and Venetian lace. The Irish Cluny lace is a pattern of cotton. Cluny lace follows the crochet stitch with a light and airy look.

Irish christening robes can feature exquisite lace in an elegant design. Vertical lace can create distinct, deeply scalloped 'panels' on a skirt - each with different enhancements. A cross decorated with broken ribbons and lovely flowers can be breathtaking on the center front. The side panels should have formed the lace in a Celtic style, and the hem would be more lacquered.

Linen from Europe

Linen is a rare cloth that has, for thousands of years, been produced from raw flax thread. Linen is woven worldwide and is a strong and resilient fabric. Irish linen is known as the world 's best linen with its skilled spinning, weaving, and finishing. Ulster, Ireland's fine linen, is a staple for Celtic baptismal fashions with bonnets, pads, and booties. Pure Irish linen can be decorated with small, sticky Celtic nodes, a row of shamrocks or rosebuds, and lovely pearls.

A beautiful Irish silk robe with a elegant Venice bead and shamrock lace with a sticky Celtic cross with trinity ties and shamrock patches is a treat. An Irish linen baptismal tower may have crosses and core at the hemline of the scalloped Victorian lace. A beautiful little panty package (with 'grandad' collar) and the Grandad shirt can be made of pure Irish linen.

Crochet

Crocheting often appears on Irish baptizing robes (sometimes referred to as 'robes' in Ireland). A shamrock inset, picot chains and a satin ribbon on the top, would be perfect, mercerized cotton with a touch of elegance. In the mid-19th century, crocheting was developed in Ireland.

The art was trained by women and children. The Irish had been professional enough to serve markets in Dublin, London, Paris, Rome, and New York in a couple of years. Crocheting led to family income supplementation. Some Irish people in fact used the money to immigrate to the USA.

Smocking

Celtic baptismal dresses may be informative, but in Ireland, the smoked fabric is still a longtime favorite. This simple style can reflect an air of elegance, made of fine Irish linen with detail on three pins across the hem, a lace-edged underneath the slip and matching cap. The bodice, cap, and sleeves of a smooth, smoking christening gown may be adorned with exquisite hand brotherhood.

Celtic cross

The Celtic Cross appears in Irish christenings everywhere. The Celtic Cross is a popular Irish icon. Perhaps a single Celtic Cross could stand in the center of a skirt with white shamrocks around the hem.

Crossed shamrock will rest under a Celtic cross on a bodice and on either side heirloom leaves. The hem of a christening robe will start with shamrocks and leaves. A child's baptismal breaker could have broken Celtic crosses, or his satin shoes would show a Celtic cross.

It is believed that the Celtic cross indicates the four wind directions as well as the four seasons. The oldest documented Irish high cross lies in Donegal. The Carndonagh Cross of the seventh century was part of a hermitage in the northwest of the county.

Knot Celtic

The Celtic Knot is a common accessory for Irish christening and accessories. The design of the Celtic Knot was found in the jewels of the Celts-even before Christ's time. The Celtic Node is linked with the ornamentation of early Christian temples and writings (like the book of Kells from the 8th century). This Irish emblem is intended to defend against evil-the, the more intricate the knotting, the more security it provides.

The Celtic Knot may feature on the bodice of a 3-piece, breathable sleeve with a Celtic flower lace border. Also, a blue Celtic knot can be seen on a robe. A blue and gold node is sometimes surrounded by red roses, while a hull, Claddagh, and thistles wander around the hem. The name of the baby and the date of the christening are also separated on the gown underneath a central mark. Trinity nodes may be split immediately under the neck by christening rompers around the arm.

Laddag's

The Claddagh (a sign of friendship and love) is always seen in the form of christening. A stunning baptismal gown may have a satin ribbon band on the front yok with a Claddagh submission. In fact, baptismal products using the Claddagh, such as a diamond rosary necklace, a crucifix, and a sweet claddag.

Life's Scottish Tree

The Celtic Tree of Existence is another Irish emblem that can be added to a baptismal gown. The Scottish tree of existence will carry knowledge. The icon is meant to give instructions from the gods.

Cross of St. Bridget

St. Bridget's Cross is a well-known Celtic symbol that appears on Irish baptismal vestments. Brigid's crosses are connected to Brigid of Kildare, venerated one of Ireland's patron saints. Constructed of pure Irish lace, it may have a pin tuck jacket, satin links in the back, and a bodice-bound St. Bridget's Cross.

Tara Brooch Stickery

Capes can use brothers modeled after the Tara Brooch – one of the best-known antiquities in Ireland. The real Tara, believed to have made around 1300 years ago, is a decorated

Celtic ring brooch consisting of gold, silver, bronze, amber, and glass. The brooch was discovered on the coast of Bettys town, south of Drogheda, and is now in Dublin in the National Museum of Ireland.

Capes Christening

Christening capes are popular for Irish babies, particularly the Kinsale cloak. Across years in rural Ireland, it was a custom to sport a full-length hooded robe. In reality, cloaks can still be seen in County Cork 's west town.

Spirals Spirals

Massive spirals flow over Irish Christian gowns gently. Prominent in ancient Ireland artifacts, Celtic spirals are the second most frequent symbols of the Celtic art to knotwork designs. There's already some ambiguity around their significance without some published information of spirals. It was prohibited in the Druid religion to compose sacred material. Spirals, of course, embodied a holy aspect for the Druid men.

Most scholars believe that spirals are symbols for the spiritual balance of the inner and outer consciousness, the sun, and the cosmos because of their simplicity. Some Celtic art scholars claim that the value of the spirals may be guided towards them. Spirals in the clockwise direction can be associated with the sun and with earth harmony. Counter-clockwise spirals could be linked to nature manipulation. Many assume that the Celtic spiral symbolizes the life seasons and time periods.

Within ancient grave mounds and holy sites, Celtic spirals are still used. Many believe that spirals have magical abilities, which keep evil from reaching a holy grave. In 1991, at the Arizona State University, archeologist Kate Johnson performed computational analysis of the arrangement of many Celtic spirals contained in ancient rock carvings. He contrasted these spiral phenomena with observational occurrences in the last millennium. His work reveals that during complete eclipses of years ago, the Celtic spirals were precise depictions of apparent celestial structures and the brightest fixed stars.

The Triskele is a three-way spiral, often used as a foundation for more complex spirals. Some claim that ancient Celtic triskeles depicted the three-year-old Triple Goddess. The Holy Trinity icon emerged later to represent God, the Father, the Angel, and the Holy Spirit of Christendom. The motif is based on the number "3," which in many ancient cultures is known as sacred.

CHAPTER FOUR

Vintage Crochet Patterns

Do you want to use antique crochet patterns? I love to look through the old magazines and see all the different applications of crochet hooks and work with wool, thread and cloth, yeah that's true. I still recall a rag guy coming to our house to buy a pound of old clothing. He wore a scale and paid a pound for it.

They appear to have taken longer than to personalize their houses. Not because today, we don't place our own personal touches in our houses, but how many days will you see a hot crochet pad in your kitchen today? A beautifully crocheted tablecloth or chair arm on the dinner table and head covered with a lovely crochet filet pattern? The doilies were still decorative and perfect for the maker.

Crocheted curtains, potholders, shelves, pats, and table runners were there. My favorite was a luxurious bedspread. That is not to mention the clothes that women created for their families during the past days.

I want this segment for free crochet antique designs. There is so much history and beauty to find and share in the crochet past. We do not want the habits to be lost by generation. Any of the old practices can be somewhat ambiguous due to their abbreviations. And hopefully, in these situations, this guide will help a bit.

bgr....beginning of rnd

ac....across

bt....between

Bl.......Block

chlp...chain loop

Ch.....Chain

Dc..... Double Crochet

D tr.....Double Treble

dec....decrease

Dec....Decrease

h d tr....half double treble

Dtr.....Double Treble

h tr....half treble crochet

H dc....Half Double Crochet

hdtr....half double treble

Hdc....Half Double Crochet

inc....increase

Inc.....Increase

indl....inclusive

Incl.....Inclusive

ltr....long treble

kcl...knot chain loop

o.m.....open mesh

O.....Thread or Yarn Over

pa....pineapple

P.....Picot

pc....popcorn st

pc popcorn stitch

prr....previous rnd

pcl....picot chain loop

r....ring

pt....point

Rnd.....Round

rf....repeat from

s.m.....solid mesh

s st.....Single Stitch (sc)

scp....scallop

Sc ....Single Crochet

Sh....shell

sec....section

Sl st.....Slip St

sk....skip

Sp.....Space

slp....small loop

Sts....Stitches

St(s)...Stitches

Tr tr....Triple Treble

Tog.....Together

x st....treble cross stitch

Tr.....Treble

Yo.....Thread or Yarn Over

Vintage Crochet Patterns - As Old as Time

Crocheting, I guarantee that before you knew of it. It's a passion as old as time; most people have. It has been around for years, and the hobby began back in the 1500s! Unfortunately, little evidence was ever given as to where it emerged.

Have you really wondered how because when that hobby began? Under the September 1997 newsletter of the American Crochet Guild, a scientist thought that crochet work could be found in Italy as far ago as the 1500s. There is no concrete justification supporting this statement, however.

Even still, we can only guess for the longest time this art has been around. And from producing home decorations to cutting clothes and other fashion accessories, it has grown.

Reminiscence

You can do a lot of things from crocheting. There are several choices to choose from, from small pockets to coats and sweaters. Yet there are still several hobbyists hunting for the iconic trends commonly seen at the beginning of the 1900s or perhaps earlier. To help you find these hard-to-look trends, certain links can be found in the World Wide Web.

-- Knit antique designs. The owner of this website, Tabitha Gibbons, sells many collections of crochet pattern books. She markets a wide variety of crochet designs, ranging from small doilies, rugs, afghans to bedding, and table cloths. You will fill in the name and email address to obtain a free pattern book by visiting their website.

-- Crochet Shrubs. It is the motto of its website with a series of classic patterns: "Patterns from the past; making heirlooms for tomorrow...' It is a member-based website that gives its subscribers over 950 antique designs. It also provides nearly 25 free antique crochet designs for personal use to guests. Nevertheless, prospective entrants are not generally approved until more notice from the holders.

-- Celt's lace antique. The antique crochet platform has a number of retro designs from which to pick. And the great thing about this platform is that they are all free of charge! It also presents the completed projects of the owner, most of the doilies as well as other table accessories.

-- Good thoughts. - Soft. With its collection of over one thousand vintage crochet patterns, this site brings you back to the past. The styles are divided into various groups – dresses, coats and slippers, hanky tops, potholders, roses and ruffles, garments, and other decorative items for the home. Through subscribing to the web, any of these designs can be displayed and reproduced. There are also some free patterns for visitors to gain a picture of the site.

-- Classic Crochet e-book examples. This kind of e-book has 20 gorgeous antique designs that can be quickly crochet and touch on fairs and bazaars. Examples of the patterns available include the lace bag, the beaded doily, and the bedspread wedding ring. It is a compact paper (pdf) file that you can access from the Crochet and Knitting site free of charge.

-- 1800's Vintage Pattern links to early 1900's. This blog, developed by a lady called Martha, also known as StarGazer, has many ties to patterns built from 1800 to the 1930s. These patterns can be freely accessed. The site also provides links to other websites offering vintage crochet patterns.

-- Traditional forms of crochet. This section on the Knitting-Crochet website has about a hundred antique patterns categorized into baby pieces, men or ladies' wear, slippers, tables, doilies, and much more. It also offers to convert your crochet knitting patterns and vice versa. Best of all, these designs can be downloaded and reproduced for personal use!

-- Traditional forms of crochet. This is different from the site above since it is not just a portion, but the name of the site itself. This platform sells antique crochet designs from the 1850s to 1950s, and all of these are baby pieces such as bonnet, booties, scarf, sweater, afghan, and a lot more. It also provides free lessons for the hobbyists and beginners.

There are just a handful of hundreds of web sites that sell hard-to-find antique designs. These places and tools will definitely bring you back in time with the great conventional trends they deliver, be it free or fee-based.

You should seriously recommend trying out these online tools when you are a crochet hobbyist. You will be able to find a wide variety of patterns both for free and for purchase. Whether you are a crochet master or a beginner for this eloquent sport, you can definitely enjoy these designs in many respects.

The Ideas Behind Crochet Patterns

Fashions change every year, but the shades still follow the same patterns. Spring and summer call for bright and fresh colors while in autumn and winter, browns, blacks, and darker colors are normally screamed.

Those accessories transform the boom into fresh insanities for modern fashions. Some of this modern crazy stuff are crochet designs. Remember that crochet patterns were only for coasters and teapot coverings for the first time.

Forget the old school designs for chairs, side tops, and even coasters. The mode is all about creativity and the desire to look amazing and set a pattern. It is a cheap and quick way to make plain patterns look fantastic.

Ideas for a basic crochet design might be ideal as designing a pair of jeans to give someone else an individual and creative feel. A crochet design will make a perfect, beautiful handbag using colors of fashion that you can alter over the seasons. Why not finish the outfit with a flower on a jacket to give that finishing detail.

Patterns can come in various sizes and types, depending on what you choose. The crochet designs are often in the shape of animals or flags. To the more patriotic of us, shades with the desired result may be combined with the yarn.

There are so many crochet designs in magazines and websites. Thousands of templates are available, but you can find great creative patterns using your own imagination, which nobody else has.

Not only are women able to take advantage of crochet styles, but it also contains several designs for kids' clothing and men's garments in tough times. Why not personalize yourself with a pattern for winter coats, gloves, and scarves as well as light jackets in summer? Men may use patterns for jacket arms patches or launch a new trend, for example, on cycling jackets and bowling tops.

There are antique styles available to women in the winter months in the form of scarves, capes, and individual coats.

Creating a crochet pattern will be pretty simple if you learn basic crocheting and various stitches. Everything you need to complete the item is the yarn and the right size hook for your pattern.

It would be a smart idea to sketch it on paper first and make your own crochet pattern. When the drawing is done, you can carry the pattern to your favorite yarn store for guidance on the right yarn and colors. Make sure you have the correct yarn weight as this will determine whether or not the item can be expanded.

If you're new to crochet, try some already finished patterns before experimenting, to experience the thickness and weight of the yarn, before you venture into more complex designs and create patterns for yourself.

The most successful way to learn design techniques is through books that can be found at reasonable prices on the internet that occasionally even free!

These sources show the designs and stitches involved and how to do it so that everybody can practice a little bit.

Many patterns still exist in charities and in shopping malls. Specialty shops typically have a large product range. Start going to the store to pick a cloth before you buy the pattern to sense the weight to texture. This will help you get home and begin to crochet.

Mind the earlier coasters and table mats? Why not turn them into a statement of fashion? This can be used for casual wear and becoming all sorts of fashion items; just use creativity! Why buy it off the shops if you're doing it yourself and for twice the price at home?

Yes, I'm not pretending that it's easy and fast to use crochet patterns and learn a new hobby, but all your hard work will certainly pay off when you compliment your personal style. Nobody else will ever look the same, even if they use the same pattern as every piece is completely unique. The modeling possibilities are infinite, with a little creativity and strong hands!

Crocheted patterns and styles don't necessarily have to be brand-new, antique patterns have recently returned to popularity, and can be used any time during summer with lighter yarn and color, and winter with darker and heavier yarns. What am I to say when and how do you wear the crocheted items?

Crochet - Seven Important Crocheting Tips to Remember

We all remember the saying the Practice is fine. You will find this in crochet very true, but it doesn't take too much practice to make your stitches perfect. Enjoy your crochet, and follow these basic tips for good crocheting.

Tip 1: When you first learn to crochet, you will find that the whole process is very strange, as you must keep the hook, yarn, and work together as you try to create different crochet stitches. But it does not take long to work, stitch until it feels normal. One great idea is to start creating a load of individual

Granny squares (or a big square) to make use of the hook naturally and easily. You can even tie them together at the end and have a comfortable blanket.

Tip 2: As users crochet, the yarn is guided by your fingers; this really creates the tension in your job and determines whether or not your crochet stitching is tight!

When you look at a crochet hook, it tapers downwards as it gets closer to the actual hook, and it has different thicknesses. The farther from the hook, it becomes thicker. So if you allow your loops to go up the hook shaft, then your loops are bigger, and therefore your work will be looser. When you operate around the knot, the loops are longer; the longer the loops, the tighter the stitches are. So if you work along the hook shaft and not near the hook, take the loops down to the hook, and pull the yarn again, so that they decrease in size.

Often tightening your stitches even further is important. Just pull your crochet yarn back at the end of the stitch.

Crochet tension is important, particularly for clothing in most crochet projects. The size of the finished garment is dictated by stress. The thinner the thread, the smaller the pin, the smaller the final product and vice versa would be. Check your crochet tension against the pattern to make sure the finished piece fits correctly. Alternatively, start crocheting where tension, such as a mat, a shawl, or Granny Square, is not important.

Tip 3: Always take the time to prepare a practice swatch when making projects where tension is essential. At the start of a project, this time will save you time and heartbreak later. (Practical swatches are always included in the patterns where applicable.) Practical swatches are just crochet pieces using the hook and yarn that the garment is made of. Patterns inform you how many stitches and rows a given length and width would be equal to.

Remember that you do not have to use the same yarn or crochet pattern size hook. The size of your crochet hook can vary when the tension is too tight, or too loosely for the particular crochet pattern. Only be careful to check tension with crocheting the practice swatch to double-check scale for a particular thickness yarn or a different size ring. This is necessary only when making some crochet clothing.

Tip 4: Relax and enjoy your crochet; your job will really show. Tip 4: Do not keep your hook or thread too close or too loose. Check back at the stitches to make sure they all have the same scale. Try to let your crochet hook move freely and automatically tighten the yarn after finishing every crochet point.

Tip 5: Keep your work always. Your thumb and forefinger will keep your crochet just below the point.

Tip 6: When attaching new yarn balls, always do so in a chain stitch and try to make sure that you crochet a straight line at the end of a row because it makes it easier to tie in the yarn ends. This will also lead to a more professional conclusion.

Tip 7: Because of its many eyelashes, crocheting with fun fur is not easy. This isn't easy for a novice because these eyelashes make it very difficult to see your crocheted stitches in reality. If you cannot see your stitches, it is very hard work and can be very frustrating to correctly position your hook in the back and front of the stitches. And it's really easy to go wrong.

If you add a second ball of yarn from a different type (any type without eyelashes) to the fun pelts at the same time and crochet with a strand of each yarn, you will visible your stitches much more easily. That makes the yarn and thus works even denser, so make sure that a garment always suits and changes the hook sizes accordingly.

Crochet Form and Function

A grandmother always stayed at the kitchen table, crocheting when her grandson was a very young child. She would also use a delicate cotton thread on a loop that had such a little head that you almost couldn't tell. grandson would wonder at the way her hands went back and forth naturally, and as if through chance, beautiful lace would emerge under her fingertips. Even as an adult, he knew that the incredible power of her agrarian hands made her seem so delicate.

She will give him the most exquisite dresses, shoes, suits, and jumpers. We felt so stunning that they were always itchy. He say they searched for and escaped into the closest puddle, itchy. The yarns of the past have often been tough. There is considerable beauty to deal with crochet. The way the thread rotates and twists around allows you to see it transform into something more. The transformation from the plain to the complicated cloth is exquisite.

There is more than a mere switch. A plain cotton thread string has so little elasticity, and yet the finished fabric stretches. This form of donation makes the fabric complete and relaxed. Crochet is a lines and spaces' visual sculpture. This fills the open areas with distorted and formed tendrils. This balance of lines and spaces makes it suitable for all seasons. This is true because body heat, based on the stitch density and type of yarn, is both trapped and released.

The characteristics of the crochet itself are perfect for Afghan construction. How many times have you been freezing and snuggled in the warmest throw, which you will still consider 20 minutes later inconveniently sweaty? You 're in a cycle of becoming cold and frustrated by the blanket again. Or worst, you 're very cold because you just can't keep heated no matter what you do, and your feet feel like 30 pounds blocks of cement. The solution to the question is crochet afghans. If the right yarns are used, the body heat can be maintained without overheating.

This low-tech art form is the perfect defense for one of the most severe diseases, a sudden syndrome of infant death (SIDS). Along with the Centers for Disease Control (CDC), the Consumer Product Health Panel (CPSC) has suggested that mothers put their infants in bed in a sleeping bag without needing to attach bedding. The reasons for this decision are obvious.

A total of 25% of SIDS deaths annually are associated with overheating and/or asphyxiation from the bedding. Children are unable to adjust their own body temperatures badly and can not adjust their heads after they work under bedding.

Well-meaning parents who are ready to wrap their babies to hold them safe also use blankets constructed from closely-knit fabrics.

The airflow is limited in densely woven fabrics. Limited airflow causes the baby to build up lost body heat and can cause the child to overheat. The infant has little power or agility to intentionally free his body from under the sheet. In the extreme, this circumstance keeps the brain temperature dangerously high and leads to death.

Limited airflow is also responsible for the second facet of bedding. Children also tend to crawl beneath bedding, and their ears are hidden with a scarf. Often, as children are powerless to get rid of themselves once anything happens, they become ultimately stuck. When they exhale carbon dioxide, it builds up near the nose and mouth of the blanket and falls under oxygen. Death by asphyxiation can be the tragic result.

No rational parent wants to jeopardize their infant, but it can be a big undertaking to battle the urge and cultural practice to unite an infant. It's a needless war. The marvel is that it can maintain warmth and allow positive airflow with all its spaces when proper yarns are used. There is no risk to the child of strangulation with the necessary stitches since the gaps are too small. (Premature babies require smaller safety dogs.) In economic terms, crochet afghans are the point of equilibrium between parental instinct and infant safety.

At Fresh from the Forest, our Grandma's Love Afghans collection provides a wide variety of baby Afghans of 46 inches and 46 inches generously. Wrap your baby in the love of Grandma.

In brief, (I realize it's a little late for this), the latest yarns available now have completely increased crochet capacity from the technically impressive to the overall kit.

How to Crochet the 4 Corners Coaster

The design of four corners is simple and convenient to crochet. Yeah, a new crochet novice will learn it quite quickly. And you can fashion a scarf, a little bag or even a full-size Afghanistan with this free crochet template.

This coaster 's finished scale is 4 inches long. There are four open holes at the edges, which make it appear amazing.

You will have to collect your materials to get started. You need just a tiny quantity of used thread. I will use a cotton thread to create a coaster. But if you create an Afghan square, you can use almost any weight yarn that you have on hand.

You need a H/8-5.00 mm for your hook model.

You'll allow a knot slip on your crochet hook to continue crocheting and allow 4 links. Join the last chain to a small circle in the first chain.

Round 1: chain 1, function in each chain two single crochets. (To make things harder, you can also operate 8 single crocheters directly in the circle.) Enter a slip in the first single crochet. (8 rendered stitches)

Round 2: Chain 1, 2 half double crochet in and across the same loop in each direction. Enter in the first thread with a slip thread. (16 rendered stitches)

Round 3: Channel 1, 2 half double crochet stitch, 2 half double crochet stitch in next two stitches, two half double crochet * next stitch, two half double crochet in next three stitches, two half crochet chain; repeat from * to last stitch, slip the last stitch. Connect the end of the first thread with a slip thread. (24 stitches and four gaps in chain-2)

Round 4: Chain 1, half twice as stitch crochet as joint, half twice in next five stitches, * 7 half twice as crochet in chain-2, half twice crochet in next 6 stitches; repeat from * up to the last chain-2 space; 7 half twice crochet in the last chain-2 space. Enter in the first thread with a slip thread. (52 made stitches)

Round 5: Chain 1, single crochet in and about the same thread. Join in the first single crochet with a slip stitch. Clamp off and weave in the ends (52 stitches made).

The crochet coaster may look a little ruffled, but it will remain like that until you flatten it a little with your fingertips. And it's big enough to have a cup of coffee.

Then you can use your recycled yarns if you use this template to knit an Afghan. If you join, however, I 'd choose a neutral color that works with all the colors you used to make your squares. And there are several ways to enter the sites. A simple single crochet always seems nice, but the flat-braid or any similar technique works as these edges are a little round.

CHAPTER FIVE

Crochet Supplies

I know of a couple, crochet varieties that are more widely used, and are named Crochet in the West, and have a broad range of methods utilizing hook and thread and loops; stitches with names such as slip stitch, chain stitch, double crochet stitch, half and third, and more.

Archeological studies indicate that Arabia is the first region in which a needle and hook operated thread. Ancient Egyptian findings indicate a professional application of hooks or needles, dating back to 950BC – 1200BC.

Throughout its history, Crochet, a word of the French word croc, meaning hook, is thought to have been made by men and women. A method that can be used to sit stand, lying or on the go, use various forms of yarn, linen, cotton, silk, and wool including finely spun and spunk precious metals (silver, gold), with or without including beads and spangles, to manufacture cloth, jewelers, pockets, rugs, furniture toppings, to create warm to light clothes, to t The hypothesis that Crochet may have been in continual usage in the Middle East for thousands of years is supported by identical crochet designs found in India and North Africa.

Tunisian or Afghan crochet or knitted crochet, worked using anything like a cross between such a hook and a needle, where and when would it first surface? Is it Tunisia? This crochet form that could really look like Crochet, knitting or weaving, was the forefather of every one of these fabric forms?

Slip crochet thread, perhaps the first way to produce Crochet and cloth.

Broom-stick crochet sometimes named pavilion thread, when and where did it come from? Was it made by the Europeans who traveled through the Americas in covered vehicles, had broomsticks and hooks, had the skills they had gained, got them out of their home countries, had very warm bedding and clothes required, started making it quickly and easily and took up crochet forms?

Irish Crochet, classic Irish Crochet, a luxurious 3-D yarn, typical of a network of chain stitching, with picots called filling, feminine and romantical, and elegant, with their elevated crocheted petals, flowers, and leaves. In Irish Crochet, a subgroup sometimes called Baby Irish crochet is continuously worked in squares or circular sections. Throughout the 1870s, Crochet became the refuge for many of the Irish people, when 12,000 to 20,000 Irish girls and women created crochet lace to raise money and help their communities through and past the potato famine.

Bruges Crochet, a lace created from triples and chain stitches, ties together the crochet ribbons to make a transparent tape like lace.

I need to know more about this national crochet Bavarian crochet, fresh to me.

Aran Crochet is identical to Aran's knitting and shapes a cloth with raised areas that are square.

Filet crochet, or crochet net, was very common in the 1920s-50s, because of its basic mesh structure and lace designs, it is easy to use charts.

Hairpin crochet was believed to be developed by ladies who used their hairpins and hooks in the Queen's Victorian period to produce a modern type of Crochet used in fine lines and triangular laces to make the tilting smoother. We replaced today the pins with looms that are conveniently adjustable in size, making it simpler to work this crochet design.

Revival during the sixties when citizens decided to function modern type clothes, by hand, in non-conforming shapes and colors, in keeping with the standards of today.

Acquards, Stripes, patchwork, knitting, clothing, looping, knit, beaded, triangles, loops, now, scrambled, Crochet is a living art that is reborn, reinvented and used in new ways using new materials that seem to be limitless. How and how individuals across history and the globe have been able to fulfill their own needs, gain money, feed their family, clothe themselves and their children, build new items, satisfy their own needs.

Crochet in the early 21st century finds it is experiencing a modern resurgence in the production, recycle, recycle and rediscovery of ancient styles, the creation of new patterns and applications, the manufacture of decorative objects, personal clothing, and artwork.

Crochet styles are changing, and Crochet is still alive.

Gayle Lorraine Gayle Lorraine Models,

New silk artwork, Victorian Superfine Merino, Merino, Alpaca, Angora plus, Silks, Cashmere, Acrylics, Glinting Floss, and Beads, making stylish pieces of fine textiles.

Eastern technology meets West, color, line, texture & balance, which are essential in fine arts and crafts, be the work 1.2 or 3D. Gayle paints on canvas and felt, stylish felt felt felt, Nuno, Cobweb and felt calamari, fabric spins, loops, Tunisian (Tricot, Afghan), broomstick crochet Irish crochet and plenty of simple Crochet.

Gayle likes easy board to make different forms of producing felt and Crochet, designing vivid, elegant, trendy, feminine, clothes, and accessories that you want to wear and own.

Vintage Crochet Is Easy

Simplified six simple stitches of crochet

Chain crochet- A chain stitch is the beginning of a project. The stitch line of the chain is the foundation of the template. Add now a knot about one inch from the yarn 's edge. Leave a loop long enough to quickly take the point of your crochet thread. Place the hook in the loop and tie the thread around the hook before removing the string. This is your first series, and now you repeat the number in the sequence. The chain stitch is the start of almost any template.

The slip stitch is typically used to bind two parts of crocheted work together. Sl or slip crochet. To shape a circle, in the style of the circular kind. Create a break, bring your crochet hook into the first stitch of your thread at the other end of the chain. Place the yarn over the thread, then draw the needle back into the crochet tube with the yarn cord. Unfortunately, both ends of the crocheted row are connected.

Sc or single crochet-Place your crochet hook in the next thread to shape this pattern. Place the thread across the lace once and loop it. You will now have two loops on your ring. Wrap the yarn around the loop, and drag the yarn off the handle. One crochet is made.

Hdc or Half-double crochet – Tie the thread around your crochet hook and create half-double crochet until you bring it into the next row. Run the thread back around the hook and take out the loop. Three loops will be on your crochet ring. Place the thread around the crochet once and remove the three loops on the crochet. Half-two crochets are made.

Dc or Double crochet- Take double crochet and loop the thread around the hook and put it into the next stitch. When the hook is in the thread, loop the rope around the hook and draw it around the thread. You've got three loops remaining on your line now. Yarn over the line and put it through the thread over the first two chains. Now two loops are on your lace pin. Wrap the yarn across the ring and draw the two strings over the line. There is double crochet.

Tr, Treble, or Quad crochet- Thread the thread twice around the crochet hook to a quad crochet stitch and then move it into the next stitch. Wrap the thread around the loop and drag it in. Four loops will be on the ring. Wrap the yarn again around the hook and pull two loops from the end. Begin to tie the yarn around the hook and drag it into two loops until a thread is on the line. Triple crochet is made.

Now that you see all the abbreviations, you know what any stitch does to the object you create. These are a few words you will know to render the correct scale, etc. There are asterisks, percentages, parentheses:

ASTERISKS (*) are used to signify that the specified number of times will be replicated for a set of stitches or moves. For, e.g., one fM, one fM, one fM from * across indicates you 're making one single crochet, one double crochet, one single crochet, up to the end of the path.

GAUGE refers to the number of stitches or rows in a specified location. Each collection of instructions describes the designer's measure while the designer worked with the specified yarn and hooks and is the gage on which the instructions are centered.

PARENTHESES) (is used for the inclusion of instructions for larger sizes as described at the beginning of every guideline. We can also indicate that the set of stitches we contain will replicate the number of times listed.

Now choose the correct crochet hook to create the object I've picked. The first of the sequence should show the needles or hooks as follows:

Loops OTHER Loops STEEL

U.S. English mm Letter

2....1 2 1/2....D

1....0 2.......B

4....2 3 1/2....G

3....1 1/2 3.......F

6....3 4 1/2.... I

5....2 1/2 4........H

8....4 6.......K

7....3 1/2 5........J

10...5

9....4 1/2

12...6

11...5 1/2

14...7

13...6 1/2

Today we mention YARNS AND THREADS, while we are mostly associating wool yarn with knitting and crocheting cotton threads, of example, the yarn or threads may be made of either natural or synthetic fabric. The synthetics are also machine washable, which are particularly valuable in products, such as baby clothes, which need regular washing.

The weight of the yarn is determined by the style of the product you make. At the start of a pattern, the form of yarn to use and the colors of certain pattern yarns are told. If the finer hooks are used for a delicate soft impact, lighter weight cotton yarns or threads are typically used. Heavier models should be used with a bulkier appearance with bigger hooks. Should not substitute any yarns if at all necessary, as such guidelines have been written for the specified yarn for calculation of the scale of the garment. Often obey the instructions of your design, and your crocheted piece is an object you treasure.

Tunisian Crochet

Instructions for Tunisian Crochet

If you've ever wanted to knit or crochet, then you probably heard about something called Tunisian crochet. In this chapter, we will talk about some context and some suggestions for using Tunisian crochet directions.

A particular type of crocheting varies in many important ways from traditional crocheting and knitting. We should cover some of the simple Tunisian crochet directions. Tunisian crochet is viewed as a cross of knitting and crochet by the majority. The distinct fabrics produced by this specific technique are more like woven than crocheted, or knitted.

Tunisian crocheting takes place on a long loop with a stopper at the end and the thread at the other. It's like a knitting needle because it's thick. The stopper preserves the several stitches on the weapon.

Tunisian crochet is distinct from the other two types of cloth production as each row is created in two separate passes. This comes the forward transfer, where the loops are operated on to the hook and then the reverse transfer, where the loops on the back of the hook are focused on.

When you do some sort of Tunisian crochet, the job is never rotated, and the right side of the garment will still remain the right side. Another term is Afghan crochet or the Afghan stitch for this form of crochet.

This specific crochet style makes a finer knit cloth and is ideal for such items as blankets and sweatshirts.

The fabric created by this crocheted material is very warm and functions well to separate the body as this crochet type tightens the fabric together. That means, of course, that the cold elements will be kept out because there are fewer openings in which the wind can flow.

Afghan clothes (blankets) are useful because this form of crochet produces a strong blanket almost air. It ensures that it can remain warm until it becomes wet, so if you hold it dry it is a perfect isolator, be it a sweater or a jacket. A jacket made of this particular technique

Very powerful to carry under a jacket as weather protection.

Many things can be produced with Tunisian crochet directions next to a jumper. There are beautiful blankest children, shawls, rugs and even games. It is a wonderful and enjoyable stitch that can be used on several designs.

Do You Know Your Crochet Terms?

You will soon realize when you learn how to crochet that the patterns use many abbreviations. These are abbreviated crochet terms to make patterns easier to read and shorter. Everyone studying how to crochet has to recognize simple crochet words to properly decipher the instructions. Any regular crochet words and abbreviations are widely used. Many of these crochet words refer to the various stitches used in a segment of a pattern and some to colors. MC is the main color crochet term used in a pattern. CC is the secondary color or light comparison used. YO implies to loop the yarn around the hook, and CH is the chain stitch crochet word.

There are also more traditional crochet words, including sc, meaning single crochet and dc, which means double crochet. Single crochet and double crochet are only for stitching; all the words used are based around a single crochet thread, which involves putting the crochet hook onto a thread. You tie the yarn around the hook then pull the needle out into the loop. There are also half-double crochet stitches that are simplified to hdc and three-double crochet stitches. Sl is the crochet slip stitch abbreviation.

British and American Crochet Words Variations

Any of the crochet designs you might find maybe American, but some may be worldwide. Some countries use other crochet words that vary elsewhere. For e.g., American and British patterns differ in a variety of crochet words. The key distinctions are significant since if the contrary meaning is used, they will alter a trend entirely. The Us slip-stitch word is considered simple crochet in the UK. The American single crochet in Britain is double crochet. Similarly, American double crochet is treble crochet, and the American triple crochet is British double-treble crochet. It's crucial for people who know how to crochet and to use various designs to recognize precisely what country words are used. The American terms could ruin the entire project with a British pattern, and vice versa. Most patterns will show where they come from or what crochet jargon they are using, so it cannot get too complicated as long as caution is taken.

Crochet Waffle Headbands and Crochet Beanie Hats - Everything You Need to Know Before You Buy

Eeny, meeny, moe, how are you ... Crochet headbands shopping and beanie hats?

When a new mom buys crochet headbands and crochet beanie caps for her baby, there are several queries. Two of the more common are: How do I recognize the size I need? Which shades am I supposed to use? Why should I add a headband to a bow or flower clip? Would I have to pay now for it to be "interchangeable

Many of us know the answers to these questions for a mom who has girls now, but for the first time, women or even women of all people, the responses aren't as obvious.

One of the biggest items to remember is selecting the right size for your crochet headbands and beanies. Crochet headbands are distributed in a number of widths and lengths. Crochet headbands are usually sold in diameter. 1.5 "to 2.75" to 3 "crochet headbands are the width of the headband and is appropriate across both ages. Width is favored only. Our strongest advice is to have a peek at photos of kids with all sizes so that you may determine the style you want for your own child. 5" and 6 "headbands are usually used by older girls and adults, which may be used with crochet beanies. Then lace beanies consisting of 6 "headbands suit 12-18 months

The second aspect that should take into account is the duration of the headbands. Some businesses sell infant crochet headbands, as well as conventional crochet headbands, and are designed in order for infants should match by adults. It may be daunting with a mother that has not bought crochet headbands. Infant headbands usually range about 4."5 "to 5."

Another problem on the buyer's face is the variety of colors. How many colors will you buy? Which colors do you need more often? Sadly, the solution to this query doesn't vary specifically from person to individual. Nevertheless, the most common colors used are whites, blue, purple, chocolate brown, and black.

Don't you know how to tie a boom to a crochet headband or hat? Don't be puzzled! You 're not alone. Some of the most popular queries we receive are: how do I add a hair bow or flower clip to my crochet headband? It's incredibly easy and quick. The crochet headbands come from cotton material that includes holes.

Sources for Carrie Crochet purchase

Crocheting returns now as a great hobby for most people, particularly those who stay at home. There are thousands of various activities that hobbyists can do with crocheting over a long period of time.

One of the variations of crochet products even in your famous shops is the crochet carriage. It's difficult to define in particular, what Carrie crochet is. There are online shops and fashion shops where items named Carrie are crocheted. There is also a different page on Carrie's crochet items. Nevertheless, they are all nice finds, so crochet hobbyists may want to look at them to see how they can create more.

Below are some of the crochet products contained in the World Wide Web by Carrie:

-- Carrie Hat Crochet. This basic and elegant hat is constructed of 100% cotton yarn by hand. Its head is only plain with the rainbow pattern on the border. This totally hides the eyes, which makes this trendy. There are three shades-beige, purple and pastel gray. This stylish hat can be bought for $19.99 from Headcovers Unlimited.

-- Carrie pack. This elegant red and silver bag is made from the festive type of yarn. This template was developed by the team of Daily Knitter and is accessible on your website. This is not intended for sale, however, but instead a pattern is provided.

-- Carrie Cotton Children's Crochet. Small Lids ended up with children's lines in spring and summer. One is this cotton crochet hat carrier that has a snuggle style. It is absolutely handmade with a light, fluffy cotton thread. This flower hat with ruffles would certainly look perfect in your little girl.

-- Carrie Sweater of Fossil. Fossil has its own sweater version of a crochet carrie. This fashion clothing elegantly crocheted has a 6-button opening and a ribbon. This is offered in three shades – bracken, safari and black silver oak. Extra small to extra-large sizes are available. You will have this at $54 from Fossil.

-- Say Carrie Corset Crochet. Yet another famous fashion company has its own crochet carriage. The tan-colored corset is handmade and filled with ramie-cotton. The top corners have a rectangular collar with flower lace patterns. This covers in front with a lace belt tied to the bottom. This corset is basic but elegant in three sizes-mini, medium and big. The demand for this exquisite dress is CAD $69.25 from the online store of Guess.

-- The Crochet Page of Carrie. This page describes Carrie's yarn selling designs. A range of caps and shawls are available from $20. Pillowcases, mattresses, and rugs are available in different colors and styles. Sweatshirts for men and women are also affordable, varying from $45 to $55. Most bed covers in crocheted are black and white and have diamond designs. They are definitely great improvements to your space and the whole home.

You won't be disappointed in choosing crochet designs since every piece can be special. Anyone who learns how to do it would surely not be disappointed with the same things again and again as thousands of designs from different sites such as the internet or handicraft books are practically available.

Crochet Source

In reality, more and more people are getting interested in this hobby. Yet do you know where and why this activity originally began?

Some papers are written about the history of this not-so-easy-to - learn needle project. But almost everybody doesn't know precisely when crocheting first began. It may be challenging to find the origins of this activity.

Nevertheless, some literature indicates that crochet may have spread from Chinese needlework to Europe in the 1700s. But many still assume that it could begin as early as the 1500s.

Nevertheless, since crochet began, the arts and crafts movement is now making its mark and gaining popularity among most people around the globe.

CHAPTER SIX

Free Winter Drifts Bracelet Crochet Pattern

Crochet bracelets are so affordable and easy to whip together that they are a great gift for young girls and adults. This design of the bracelet is really simple to crochet to every scale, making it possible to crochet in any content.

The bracelet is designed to slide around the wrist so that you don't have to grip it. So, most kids will be healthy so secure.

The level of expertise for this pattern is: easy / medium.

Your resources collection includes:

Yarn: Red Heart Super Saver # 4, Plus 3 plus 10 Crochet Thread Length

Hook: H/8-5.00 mm for # 4, Size 3 G, and Size 10 1.65 mm for # 4.

The completed proportions are as follows: they weigh about 3,5'' in dimension. They can also be modified to any size if appropriate.

This design illustrates how the bracelet is crocheted in one color. However, it is simple to introduce a little more color as the second round switches to a different color.

In used yarn and with H hook:

Loosely chain 22 (or multiples of 2), apply a slip point to the first chain so as to prevent twisted links.

Round 1: Chain 1 in the bends, one single crochet in and across the same thread; apply a slip stitch to the first single crochet. (22 points)

Loop 2: Chain 1, with the same stitch as a link (single crochet, triple crochet) in the next stitch (single crochet, triple crochet), repeat with a * line; connect a slip stitch in the first crochet. (22 points)

Round 3: chain 1, single stitch crochet in and around each stitch; first stitch slip stitch. (22 stitches) Fly down.

In Size 3 Thread and G Crochet Hook: Chain 30, follow the above instructions.

For a size ten thread and a steel hook of 1,65 mm: Chain 56, obey the directions above.

To order to make a tailor-made necklace, just raise or decrease the stitches to either of the two.

I think you'll use this design for the crochet bracelet. It works quickly, and you just need a limited amount of thread, and it won't cost you much more than a few minutes.

Happiness End the Rat Race

End the Council Race

Life must come to an end, like all wonderful holidays. While some may consider this opening line as a depriving feeling, I hope others would also consider it as sobering.

Life is a temporary thing, and it doesn't last forever, much like a holiday. Time and space make us all fascinated by the illusion that our death is somewhere far in the distance, and yet we all know that this is an illusion itself. Many of us get up and do the same things that we did the previous day. But what most of us fail to recognize is that we recycle our thoughts and beliefs as well.

This weekend, we said goodbye to a woman who seemed to be the one who would escape a life without ever dies. Her smile was big, and her laugh was heartfelt. She incredibly loved by her husband and two beautiful children. Her big family gathered around her during her illness, a five-year trip, but in the end, as it is going to be for all of us, she made this vacation adieu.

I'll see my friend again, perhaps not this year or the next, or maybe tomorrow I'll see her. Who knows? Who knows? But this post aims to help us realize how peculiar most of us is so that we can wake up and look every day as a valuable holiday.

Life should not be a Competition-it should be treated as a holiday.

When I find it to be a vacation, I'm more conscious of doing as much of the wondrous stuff I appreciate in it as I can to spend time contemplating, concentrating, or engaging in activities I don't like, exhausting me, frustrating me or pissing me off.

If you don't want to visit the North Pole Crocheting Museum, would you spend your time and your money booking flights, stay in a hotel and find the opportunity to visit the Yarn and Hook Museum in freezing cold conditions? Not probably ...

But for a moment, think about it.

Why do people appreciate the value of their time and money for holidays, but so much of our energies in our everyday lives are wasted on things we don't like?

How are we able to waste time investing in excursions, accommodation, and clothing, but we prefer to fall into a certain sleep cycle every day?

Why is our energy, resources, memories, and life more valuable while we're on holiday, but do not enjoy our NOW moments when we're NOT on holiday?

Do you want to go on holiday with a group of people you hated?

Would you stop to talk in the lobby of a luxurious cruise ship with energy vampires if you spent $10,000 on a 10-day journey across Europe?

Can you welcome a selfish partner to spend these important ten days with you whilst spinning in the beauty of Europe?

Of course not! Of course not!

Then why many of us spend our precious time in and dialogue that depletes us, or why do we so frequently accept our own ridiculous thinking because we realize that our life is an end of a vacation?

The solution is a little difficult.

At the same time, human beings are both conscious and unconscious. We are also creatures with instant gratification wired in their brains. Our waking mind is guided by implicit conditioning beneath the canopy of consciousness. We are programmed to do the same if we suffered childhood trauma or if our careers have conditioned us to lament, waste time, judge, criticize, and essentially do NOT appreciate that gift life is. If we are conditioned to believe that we are not sufficient, we may be seeking immediate gratification through maladaptive handling skills such as codependence. We can please people, fawn, argue, or try not to control things, situations, and people.

Most of all, people want to be loved and loved. When the fear of abandonment begins, our brain is cabled to avoid suffering and to try and get immediate satisfaction to join someone, OR maybe we want to avoid being abandoned by someone we unconsciously believe we should remain connected or may want to avoid feeling rejected.

Living Over the Veil of Conscience

Now than ever, people wake up to get to learn the rat-like mentality that has infected our consciousness. We learn to use a new lens to OBSERVE the insane tracks in our minds. We know FINALLY that feelings are only concepts, and they are NOT us. Thoughts are words strung as clothes on a line. They are the products of language, memory, emotions, experiences, and the brain's need to divide, organize, and understand what was downloaded into the subconscious.

But here's the tough part — If the update is garbage, then the data flowing through the aware sector is garbage! If you are conditioned to believe that you are indignant, guess what? You can live rat 's existence, guided by compulsions and latent emotional needs, under the veil of consciousness.

You 're not a Committee.

You 're not a rodent, and this just ought to be thrilling. You've got a choice. You will wake up and plan to invest time doing something you think would enhance your life experience. You don't have to start exhausting indoor or outdoor discussions. You can learn diving, cha-cha, painting, singing, or playing a tool. You may engage in the spiritual path, develop your professional communication skills, or return to school. You can learn how to make money, move to another country, or start a whole new business.

You 're not a dog. You 're not a guy. You are a holy, dynamic, conscious being locked in the most strong manner anyone might ever imagine. Your body is just magic! It's a sanctuary that holds the true you are.

Today, can you look at this day as a holiday and enjoy all your days as your last day.

That is the road of gladness.

Proper Maintenance of Your Garbage Disposal

Through correctly managing your waste management, your life will be prolonged, and plumbing and sanitation can be avoided.

Let's face it. Most of us have waste management, so we don't handle them favorably in our houses. Indeed, I believe that we take this household equipment for granted. A poorly maintained or operated disposal can and will disrupt, block, and block drains and cause an endless list of costly plumbing and drain disasters.

Closed drains are an inconvenience, and the repair of waste disposal can be very costly. Don't worry, and most problems are totally unnecessary. Regular maintenance and care are very easy. When you handle the waste properly, it will handle you properly.

Here are a few common practices along with the key ones to be practiced.

Disposal of waste best practices:

- Keep the waste collection clear. Pour a little dish soap inside and let it run after cleaning dishes for a minute with some cool water.
- Staff the machine on a daily basis. Disposal also helps avoid rust and decay and guarantees that all pieces stay in motion. This will also eliminate some blockages.
- Melt the food waste with a powerful cold water blast. Do you call for cool water? It allows some grease or oils that may be solidified into the device to be removed before entering the pit.
- Melt some hard material like bones of fish, eggshells, little pits of fruit, etc. This triggers a scoring motion

within the scrub chamber, which helps to clean the disposal walls.

- Boil citrus peelings like lemons or oranges to recreate the flavor of runoff.
- Cut big pieces into smaller sections. Put them one by one in the grinder, instead of attempting to fire a large number at once.
- Disposal of Materials Don't:
- Do not bring in the device something that is not biodegradable. Non-food items will damage the engine and both blades. Your disposal of garbage is not trash.
- Don't know breakwater, plastic, metal, or paper.
- Don't grind fuel at all.
- Do not grind butts of cigarette.
- Should not insert butter, oil, or grease into or empty the trash. Grease accumulates gradually and impedes the opportunity to ground and obstruct drains for the waste disposal.
- Should not use hot water for food waste grinding. Hot water allows the graft to liquefy and collect, allowing drains to choke.
- Should not smile rather fibrous things, such as celery stalks, corn husks, artichokes, and onion skin. Fibers can tangle and jam the engine and block drain from these.
- Should not shut off the engine or water until it has been ground. Switch off the waste disposal first when the grinding is complete. Let the water flow for at least 15 seconds to wash away all the residual debris.
- Don't cut too many potato peels from the trash. In the potatoes, the starches are a sticky paste, which may lead the blades to stick.
- Don't dispose of huge quantities of food. Feed food into the machine of cool water flowing a little at once.

- Don't dispose of expandable food with the garbage. Foods such as pasta and rice expand once you put water into a pot; once inside your pipes or garbage disposal, they do the same thing and cause a number of jams and blockages.
- Don't ground large bones of livestock (beef, pork, etc.).
- Although coffee grounds do not harm the disposal, over time, they will accumulate in drains and pipes.
- Should not use toxic substances such as chlorine or cleansers for drainage. Blades and pipes may be harmed. Borax is a safe sink cleaner and sanitizer that operates well on smell-causing molds and mildews.

Hold your Disposal Working Open

- Ice is an efficient and cost-effective way to clean up your waste disposal, sharpen your blades and break up any grease. Take a few ice cubes and run them into the waste disposal. When the waste disposal cuts through the ice blocks, the ice chips scrutinize certain parts of the device that are impossible to access and melt into the sink. Seek to maintain the machine in decent working order once or twice a month. To kill the unpleasant smells.

Here are some natural methods that are environmentally sustainable and really inexpensive.

- Take a lemon or orange periodically and throw it into the disposal. The oils and juices created from the fruits and peels naturally purify the walls inside the disposal and generate a new, robust fragrance.

- Freeze the ice cube trays of vinegar and toss them down. This leaves the blades clean and destroys smell-causing bacteria safely.
- For unpleasant odors, dump the baking soda into the sink and allow it to remain a few hours until water and waste are discarded.
- Use a natural cleaning drug-like Borax with very strong smells. Only dump 3-4 Borax teaspoons down the drain and wait for an hour. Switch on the hot water and wash away the borax.

Item Elimination Suggestions:

- NEVER, NEVER, NEVER, have your unprotected hand disposed of! If you have to use your hand to grab items, unplug the device, or switch off the matching breaker. Wear protective gloves also to shield the hand from sharp knives.
- If you have to challenge yourself to locate a foreign item, grab a torch, and identify the right position of the object first. To remove the piece, using an extra-long nose pin or an industrial finger gripper (available in most hardware shops). In some cases, you could use a bent coat-hanger for dislodging and hooking the object. Only a pair of chopsticks or crochet needles will operate to catch the target (yes, I know how crocheting needles are).

What to do if the waste disposal doesn't melt:

- A number of devices that do not appear to work just have to be reset. It's quick to fix your disposal. Only glance at the red or black reset button on the engine under your tub. Push reset. Push reset. Note: If the disposal of waste is attached to the outlet of the building, ensure the outlet is solid.

- A blown a fuse or tripped circuit breaker is checked.
- Give it a start-up drive. Many waste management systems have a loop below that lets you manually tie it out while it's stuck. Use an Alan clamp or garbage disposal tool to crank it in most hardware stores. Most non-serious jams should be published.

Call the plumber-If in doubt!

This is just general repair suggestions for small issues and easy solutions. If you seek these solutions and they don't fit or if the situation begins to escalate, get in touch with the plumber. We are experts, and they have the equipment and know-how to cope with virtually any waste management situation.

Crafting with Vintage Linens

As a collection, display, and decoration with handwork and textiles become more important, and it is much harder for "perfect" vintage textiles to be found. If you can find a great item, it will probably be really costly. Low than perfect vintage stickers, clothing, doilies, quilts, and coverings are easy to find and are much cheaper than their counterparts in the "mint condition." Vintage pieces were also time-testing and very long-lasting. These parts were also laundered luxuriously smooth, and fading and slight defects contributed only to their beauty. From these slightly failed pieces, you can produce a variety of new projects.

Things to search for:

Look for products that are average to decent overall. Carefully inspect the item to test for scratches, yellowing, or drops. You should also smell any part you plan to buy. Some smells will come out, like the slight mustiness of the storage. Others do not, including smoking and mildew. If the item is less than ideal, search for rescue areas. Tiny tears and tears of a handkerchief make it unusable, but the same tears and stains on a bed give a ton of good content for crafts and sewing. Don't get bothered by supposed defects like missed keys or unfinished trimmings. These items are not as usual, and their inferior shape allows you to cut them into without fault and allows you to buy items with great savings.

Any detailed details regarding the various styles of antique linen and other metrics for increasing selection:

Handcrafts:

Hankies are perfect to create smaller designs or to give a color splash to bigger ones. Handcuffs come in a wide variety of colors and designs. They can be hand- or machine-brother, printed with floral or other models, or cut with crocheted or lace edges. Kid's and souvenir hankies are often available, but collectors love them-they always cost you more than "normal" versions. When shopping for handkerchiefs, look for clean and pretty pieces in your favorite colors. Although the flawless crochet or lace rim is fun and provides more choices, hankies with imperfect rims also may be used for sewing projects.

Look for collections or individuals. The initial package will also include sets of three or four hankies. If you see your original handkerchief or anyone close you, purchase it! These are helpful when you have to attach a personal touch to a project.

Accessories are broken:

Brothered accessories such as placemats, table runners, pillowcases, and servings were often made to decorate the home. Almost always show "perfect" images such as roses, animals, and monograms and offer your retro linen creations a handcrafted touch. They may be used for small to medium-sized projects or to give bigger projects a special touch. Sticky products may be bought in groups or as individual pieces. If you design a quilt or a collection of things that suit, purchase damaged accessories in similar classes. If you're working on a particular item, such as a sweet accent pillow or necklace, you only need one piece.

Quilts, bedspreads, and covers "cutter."

For every size of Project, quilts, bedspreads, and sheets fit well. They are large enough to cover furniture, produce or support new quilts, or create matched item sets. Test the whole surface for defects when you buy these pieces. Most standard items of "cutter" or art "may have certain defects, typically tiny tears or flecks.

Quilts:

It takes a great deal of time and commitment to make a quilt. Unfortunately, quilting has not been valued for many years, and many great quilts have suffered as a result. Poor treatment, inadequate storage techniques, and shoddy care have damaged many quilts after a repair, but damaged quilts may not be suitable for the intended purpose.

"Orphan" Quilt Blocks are still accessible from a wide variety of outlets. Orphan Blocks are single quilt blocks or tiny quilt blocks, which were only used in a bigger project. It might have been determined by the initial Quilt Creator not to complete the Project and may only have leftover blocks since it was completed.

Spreads of bed:

Forms I want to buy are either antique cotton-printed spreads or spreads of the cotton canal. A large size chenille spread in the "design" condition produces approximately four yards of cloth for around $20 or about $5.00 a yard. The Latest Chenille of the same nature is about $25 a yard — a substratum for around $20 a yard.

Boards and pillowcases:

Antique sheets and pillowcases are typically cottoning that has a beautiful flower or ticking design. Sheets and pillowcases are perfect for a number of projects, particularly when the fabric is soft and cloth is a necessity. Using nice vintage sheets to help a quilt and/or to cover a jacket.

Clothing:

Vintage clothing works well for various projects. Use "special" items — cotton clothing, flannel shirts, tees, dresses, and aprons — even t-shirts — for your projects to be customized. Don't forget the details — lace, sticks, lovely buttons, smoking dress fronts, etc.

Stuff to prevent:

Your eyes and nose are the best judges to prevent - tines and odors are the biggest culprits with the old linens. Don't forget to take care of everything. Unfold and examine any item you are interested in shopping. Minor flaws can be worked around, but all pieces must be checked in order to be certain that they are in useful condition.

Look for fabrics that have been unnecessarily starched; they can sound clean when you buy them, but with starching, they may render the fabric brittle and too delicate to operate with. Products that smell bleach can be a bright white, yet they still maintain the scent of bleach after constant washing.

I also avoid using real antiques or collector items. Save these to show to accentuate your works. Antique or collectible-quality items are not the only ones costing you, but usually, they are too beautiful for you to cut into. There are so many fewer than perfect items out there, and I prefer not to cut them into an object that is collectible.

And if far less than horrible linens are salvageable, real "obscures" can be avoided. Unusable pieces contain linens with horrific or unpleasant colors, bad textures, lumpy material, massive, unattractive motifs, and textiles that look terrible to the touch. If you do not like an early piece-color, pattern, borders, etc.

CONCLUSION

Crocheting will encourage you to do a lot, from tiny bags to jackets and sweaters. There are various solutions open. Crochet design publishers also try template testers. Contact several organizations and propose trends for analysis. Crochet patterns offered by the most affordable rates and excellent production of Chinese manufacturers. Lists will properly direct you to vital details such as company description, key items, target audience, contact information, certifications, and more.

Crotchetier does not exclusively limit itself to the template instructions. It is necessary to express a personal opinion that will help to enhance the presentation of the project. These references are very helpful to those new to the hobby, but even the advanced expert can take advantage of crochet patterns. Crocheting will encourage you to do a lot, from tiny bags to jackets and sweaters. There are various solutions open. Crochet design publishers also try template testers. Crochet patterns offered by the most affordable rates and excellent production of Chinese manufacturers.

In addition to conventional knitting lessons, there are also other versions of new designs that are illustrated, and several yarn shops also sell crochet lessons. Filet crochet, Tunisian Crochet, poultry lace, crop-hooking lace, and Irish Crochet are all variants of the traditional form of Crochet. These magazines often show basic crochet designs built for beginners and even crocheters. Expert Crotchetier, who crochet designs frequently featured in art publications for a long, long time.

Anyone who crochets assures you that creating and producing a range of exquisite and totally unique items from their own two hands is simply priceless. The first pillow, first jacket, first table cover for newcomers add a pleasure that was previously unknown.

So, giving away crochet Christmas material is only one of the wonderful things you might make with Crochet. All crochet projects start with a knot of slip. Place the end of the yarn over the palm of your hand from right to right, then back over your thumb, then place it over the end of the first strand again.

Expert Crotchetier, who crochet designs frequently featured in art publications for a long, long time. Now place the thread on the crochet hook and insert it in the last string. That's how you begin every crochet project. Once put flat, it seems like a big crocheted design with a hole in the middle. Each one is quick and fast to create Afghan crocheted cover is a perfect gift for family and friends. It can be used as a scarf or shawl in the cold winters. The problem of selecting window accents with the right size or color can be solved conveniently with crochet window accent designs. The exact template or style required for your decoration might not always be readily accessible, but with crocheted window decorations, you will still find a pattern that fits or can easily be fine-tuned.

A broad range of free and commercial crochet patterns covering a large spectrum of uses are available. Changes in fashion indicate that various styles of crocheted items become common during different periods. When you're new to wire crochet, aim not too tightly; let the wire flow around your fingers easily. Without careful preparation, bead crochet bags may be made, and further freeform techniques used. Knitted and crocheted pieces continued to be common in the early 1900s? s. If you're searching for a Halloween outfit for the little one or a holiday table runner, you may also get free crochet patterns from crochet books, art magazines, and libraries. However, the Internet is a feasible alternative because all free habits can be made by sitting in home comfort.

These references are very helpful to those new to the hobby, but even the advanced expert can take advantage of crochet patterns. Many say it may be a smart idea to hold your things sorted and confined through knitting or crocheting. But presumably, you should wait before your supplies and inventory really go.